# WOMEN TO WOMEN

## YOUNG AMERICANS
## IN SOUTH AFRICA

# WOMEN TO WOMEN
## YOUNG AMERICANS
## IN SOUTH AFRICA

EDITED BY DAN CONNELL

**Africa World Press, Inc.**

P.O. Box 1892

Trenton, NJ 08607

P.O. Box 48

Asmara, ERITREA

**Africa World Press, Inc.**

P.O. Box 1892                 P.O. Box 48
Trenton, NJ 08607       Asmara, ERITREA

Book and cover design: Marleen Marino and Jackie Anderson/Studio 5,
    Simmons College
Cover photos: Dan Connell/The Image Works
Front cover art:: Copper etching on the outer wall of South Africa's
    Constitutional Court

ISBN 1-59221-450-9 (hardcover)
ISBN 1-59221-451-7 (paperback)

**Library of Congress Cataloging-in-Publication Data**

Women-to-women : Young Americans in South Africa / edited by Dan
Connell.
     p. cm.
  Includes bibliographical references and index.
   ISBN 1-59221-450-9 (hardcover) -- ISBN 1-59221-451-7 (pbk.)
  1.  Social problems--South Africa. 2.  South Africa–Social
conditions--1994- 3.  Women–South Africa--Social conditions.
4.  South Africa--Foreign public opinion, American.  I. Connell, Dan.

  HN801.A8W65 2006
  303.48'20820968--dc22

                   2005036260

*To the women
who are building
the New South Africa*

All royalties from
the sale of this book
will be donated to
charitable organizations
in South Africa.

To support these projects,
make a tax-deductible check
out to "SA Development
Fund (Simmons)" and send it to:

*South Africa Development Fund
555 Amory Street
Boston, MA 02130*

# TABLE OF CONTENTS

# ACKNOWLEDGMENTS

Many South Africans gave generously of themselves and their time to make this project possible, despite the extraordinary burdens they carry in their continuing efforts to construct a new, democratic South Africa. Some appear in these articles; many do not. Some are listed in the appendix; others are not. To all who helped, listed or not, a heartfelt thanks. Among those who opened doors, set up meetings and arranged the exposures that made this so special were: Barbara Buntman, David Andrew, Deborah Posel, Sheila Meintjes and Anton Harber (University of Witwatersrand); Bobbie Marie (COSATU); Shamim Meer and Maia Marie (friends and interlocutors); Jeremy Cronin (SACP/ANC Member of Parliament); Jim Callahan, Lou Mazel and Judith Sowerby (U.S. diplomatic staff); Paul Sedres (University of Cape Town); Vivienne Carelse (Iziko); and Thana Nell (Jedek Travel) and the two Jedek guides and guardians who traveled with us much of the time, Nkuli Simelane and Mervin Wessels.

Thanks to Simmons College dean Diane Raymond for underwriting my March 2005 trip to South Africa and for supporting the concept from the beginning; to Simmons communications department chair Jim Corcoran for brainstorming the project with me and then supporting it throughout (and afterward). Also Vito Grillo and Robin Melavalin in the Simmons study abroad office and Joanna Johnson and Joe Roma at Intrax Education Abroad for their patient work in putting together the logistical piece of the trip. And Africa World Press publisher Kassahun Checole for working to make this book a reality.

Special thanks to the crew of Studio 5, a Simmons College senior communications seminar, for the outstanding work they did in designing and laying out the book. They went way above and beyond their classroom obligations to make this a success. Among those who deserve special recognition are graphic designers Marleen Marino and Jackie Anderson and project manager Kristen Lucek, as well as their professors and mentors, Judy Richland and Sarah Burrows, and freelance copyeditor Sarah Putnam.

# INTRODUCTION

On April 26-29, 1994, South Africans held the first multiracial, democratic national elections in their turbulent history. The victory of the African National Congress with 63 percent of the ballots and the election of the country's first black president, Nelson Mandela, signaled the formal end to the draconian political system of racial domination known as apartheid. But the freedom struggle was far from over, as we found upon our arrival eleven years later.

The liberation movement's announced objective was not simply the transfer of power. It was the construction of an open, democratic society built on the principle of unity in diversity in which the basic needs of all its citizens, as well as their political rights, would be guaranteed. The challenge was as daunting as it was out of synch with much of the rest of the world—which made it all the more inspiring, even as it invited skepticism.

The new political landscape had first to be consolidated. The promise of equality had to be extended to the economic and social spheres. And a new, inclusive political culture had to be constructed to both reflect and reinforce this transformational project—one that took into account not only race, but gender, sex, pregnancy, marital status, ethnic or social origin, color, sexual orientation, age, disability, religion, conscience, belief, culture, language and birth, in the terms set out by the country's new constitution.

A bit more than a decade after the electoral transition, fifteen students from Simmons College, Boston—all women—set out to explore post-apartheid South Africa to see for themselves where along the winding road to the realization of this bold vision the society had come, particularly as it applied to gender. And whether and to what extent it was still moving in this direction. They went to observe, record, reflect and learn. As budding journalists, their brief was to communicate slices of this experience through which readers might discover something about the New South Africa and about social and political change itself.

The undertaking was part of an advanced feature-writing course, my first such student-travel project since I began teaching journalism and African politics at Simmons in 2002, but not my first visit to South Africa. That had come in early 1986 when I was the director of a Boston-based development and information agency, Grassroots International, that was supporting the anti-apartheid struggle. I had come back in the 1990s on several consultancies and research missions, the last in 1995 and 1996 to compare social and political movements in four transitional societies for a book, *Rethinking Revolution* (Red Sea Press, 2002). I visited again briefly in March 2005 to set up the Simmons visit, but for all practical purposes the May-June 2005 trip was my first encounter with post-apartheid South Africa, and I found myself learning alongside my students with a freshness and vigor that was both energizing and unrelentingly challenging. Education should always be so.

The project was a Simmons "short course"—an intensive study abroad program that runs between semesters. However, faced with the need to ground ourselves in South Africa's complicated context before we arrived, we had met frequently over the previous six months—exploring the history, delving into the rich store of apartheid-era fiction, researching magazine and journal articles, reading speeches and polemics and doing writing workshops. Much of this was done on volunteer time sandwiched between other classes and extracurricular activities, as well as off-campus employment, since many participants held part-time jobs to pay school fees, including the cost of this trip.

As a group of African Americans, Asian Americans and European Americans—rich and poor, gay and straight from diverse social backgrounds—we mirrored the South African rainbow within our ranks. Among the students were majors in communications, political science and international relations, management, nursing, chemistry and math. We had the head of the Black Students Organization, the head of the Asian Students Organization, the head of the International Multicultural Students Association, last year's editor of *The Simmons Voice*, next year's editor of *The Simmons Voice* (and the literary magazine *Sidelines*), and members of student government and a number of other activist organizations and service learning programs.

These were students who came prepared to act on what they learned—as this book indicates, and as do their continuing efforts to educate their peers and to raise funds for projects they encountered while in South Africa.

We landed in Johannesburg on Monday, May 19, 2005. Our goal was to explore the intersection of gender with race and class in the New South Africa—and to write about it from the standpoint of those who experienced it firsthand.

How, we wondered, did the promise of social equality that animated this decades-long struggle translate into the restructuring of relations between women and men—and the rethinking of gender itself? What are South African women doing now? What are they thinking about? What new issues do they face in this post-apartheid world? What aspirations do they nurture? What obstacles do they face? How do men deal with these changes? And how do these gender-focused objectives mesh with or compete against the drive for racial equality?

We departed South Africa three weeks later, after observing and talking with a parade of activists and academics, radicals and reformers, politicians and media practitioners, artists and musicians, and many, many others. We met women who work to change the world by day but must don their aprons and serve their families once at home; women who have lost everything but yet find the will to rebuild their lives, homes and communities—one brick at a time; and women who channel their considerable pain and anger into their art in a self-conscious effort to free themselves by projecting it into the public domain.

We attended plays, concerts and poetry readings that celebrated the New South Africa even as they focused attention on the ravages of unemployment, domestic violence and HIV/AIDS that have surfaced since the fight against apartheid was won. And we trundled through the streets and back alleys of the country's persistent slums and sprawling squatter camps to sit with those still left behind to hear their stories and to ponder the implications of their continuing exclusion.

We found that South Africa has achieved a great deal of progress—to the extent, at least, that the walls separating people from one another and from access to opportunities for self-advancement are becoming more porous than ever before, particularly when it comes to gender. But they are not coming down altogether. Instead, a fortunate few appear to be achieving heretofore unimaginable success while many continue to be left out.

Nowhere in Africa do women have more clearly spelled out legal rights, with a constitution that prohibits discrimination on the basis not only of gender but also of sexual orientation. The first post-apartheid parliament—presided over by a woman Speaker—boasted the seventh highest percentage of women in the world (up from 141st before the 1994 elections). But inserting women into the top of the South African pyramid was only a first step in transforming the gross inequalities the liberation movement inherited with its ascent to power—and one that ran the risk of obscuring just how far the overwhelming majority of women have to come just to reach a point where they can even participate in this newly democratized nation.

In 2005, there remain powerful impediments to reaching the top tiers of politics, business, the media and more—glass ceilings beyond which few are yet able to go. Women are well represented in parliament, for example, but not in positions of top party leadership. The trade unions have gender departments at nearly every level of organization (as does the state), but there are few women in leadership. There are nearly as many women as men in the media, but most work as production assistants and reporters and only rarely as editors or publishers. Some women are on a fast-track in business, at least as far as middle management or as proprietors of small businesses, but few are visible near the top in the large corporations that dominate the South African landscape. And this does not begin to address the plight of millions of women in the urban squatter camps and the impoverished rural areas who lack the education or skills to approach these newly opened doors.

Throughout the trip, I was reminded of an encounter I had in 1995 with a black South African camped out in a single room in an abandoned house outside Durban. His cramped quarters were plastered with ANC election posters. He took his water from an outdoor spigot he shared with seventeen others, and he cooked his meals on an open fire in the courtyard. When asked about his hopes for the future, he quickly acknowledged that the new ANC government faced a formidable challenge with far too few resources, and he said he was willing to wait for the house he had dreamed of for many, many years. "All I need to know is that I am in line for one," he added. "And that the line is moving."

A decade on, it is apparent that the grace period for the victorious anti-apartheid movement is nearing an end, as the patience of the long-suffering black majority begins to fray. During our brief stay, dozens of protests erupted in urban townships over the slow pace of housing construction and service delivery, at one point forcing our bus to seek an alternate route as burning tires blocked our passage. (Since then protestors have burned entire trains.) One week, *The Weekly Mail* put out an edition with much of the front page blacked out for the first time since the apartheid era when the ANC government blocked publication of an exposé of corruption in high places. And we repeatedly encountered individuals critical of the new regime—some of them veterans of the struggle, some not. Nowhere was the criticism more intense—and more angry—than among those dealing with the government's response to the HIV/AIDS crisis, as several of the articles in this collection reveal.

Under these circumstances, the challenge for us was to place what we saw and heard in a wider context and to communicate this framework so that readers, too, can witness this extraordinary social and political experiment as part of a complex process to be evaluated in terms of where it is coming from as well as where it is going, rather than simply measuring it against the world we know here. This would be no mean task for a veteran reporter, but it was all the more complicated for a group of young Americans also coping with the impact this was having on their personal and political identities and on their perceptions of the society from which we had come. It is left to you to judge the extent to which we succeeded.

Our most fervent hope is that we will stir your interest in and excitement about what is happening in South Africa today, which, for all its flaws and contradictions, nevertheless challenges us all to ask what we value most as individuals and as members of an open but also imperfect society and what we can do, one by one as well as together, to make it better.

*Dan Connell*
*Boston,*
*Massachusetts*
*December 2005*

# KEEPING THE PAST PRESENT

# A Tour Guide Works to Heal a Nation

By Gina Patterson
Cape Town, South Africa

Pink roses decorate a lace table setting for eighteen people. Pink and blue embroidered pillowcases line the low brown couch. Nelson Mandela's black-and-white picture hangs in the middle of the room.

Tea cups rattle as Shereen Habib points out with her delicate, light-brown hands which pot has Ceylon and which has Roibois before introducing a visiting student group to a little-known or little understood South African sub-culture—the Cape Malays.

Shereen's neutral striped scarf covers her silky black hair. Wearing a black jacket and checkered green and brown pants, she raises her arm in a sweeping motion as she tells the group that this is her home. Set in the heart of Cape Town, South Africa's most important seaport, her home is part of a close–knit Muslim community known as Bo–Kaap.

Her two-story house is different from others in the quiet residential neighborhood; tourists come in and out regularly. The founder of Tana Baru Tours, a small but successful new company, Shereen is the only tour guide in her community.

Many black tour guides in South Africa use their jobs to heal the wounds of apartheid. As a member of what South Africa calls the "colored" community–those of mixed race, many of whom trace their ancestry to

> *Using secret codes, she and her friends set up meetings to talk about how they could help the underground African National Congress.*

Indonesian slaves—Shereen does this for Cape Town Muslims.

"It was a hard time for me," Shereen says, speaking of the dark days of the apartheid era, when she was married to a Frenchman. The racist white government had made it illegal to intermarry, so she had to go into exile in the Seychelles. After a while, feeling cut off from her homeland and the fight to change it, she separated from her husband to come back to South Africa.

Back in Bo-Kaap, Shereen was again a target of the apartheid regime, as she became more and more involved in the struggle. Using secret codes, she and her friends set up meetings to talk about how they could help the underground African National Congress.

Shereen's home became a safe haven for political prisoners, including the country's current minister of finance. Some even died there. This landed her in and out of jail and often isolated her from her children, she says, looking at her eldest daughter.

In 1990, the government freed ANC leader and future South African president Nelson Mandela from jail. Shereen smiles as she describes this as the best moment in her life. After his release, Mandela was set to give a speech in front of thousands when a man ran through the crowd with a gun.

Shots flew.

"This is how far I was from being shot that day," Shereen says, indicating a spot about ten inches from her head.

"But Madiba getting out of jail was my favorite moment," she adds, using Mandela's nickname.

After the transition to the new government, Mandela toured much of South Africa, including the Bo-Kaap community. At his request, Bo-Kaap became a preserved site.

Around that time, everyone in the community painted their homes the colors of exotic flowers and tropical seas. These represented their new freedom, according to Shereen, who says that it was then that she envisioned the Tana Baru Tour Company.

Using her knowledge of the Bo-Kaap Muslim community, she started to give tours to professors and school groups. She then branched into giving tours to other visitors, South Africans and foreigners.

She smiles while talking about the friendly atmosphere in the community. And she sighs when talking about the community's latest threat—well-to-do South Africans and Europeans buying up the increasingly valuable urban property for vacation homes. Gentrification is driving prices up so that locals cannot afford the land, she says.

Shereen is deeply upset about this and wants the community to resist. On the wall hangs a large poster with her picture in the center from when she ran unsuccessfully for a parliament seat on the ANC slate.

"The ANC improved all fields and departments for people," she says, adding that she no longer aspires to political office. Today, her focus is on educating others in and out of her community.

"It is important to tell my story," she says.

"The Cape Flats were where I grew up, and I wanted to run away, but now I share my experiences because it relieves what anger and sadness I had. South Africa went through a very fast healing process. There was no time for drama; I had to take charge of education and the past history."

# TOURISM AS SOCIAL ACTIVISM

## BY EVAN KUHLMAN
## CAPE TOWN, SOUTH AFRICA

The shadows of giant buses fill the narrow streets of this tightly knit Muslim community, their tinted windows blocking the sun from the warren of one- and two-story homes that comprise this historically insular hillside neighborhood.

It is just another day for one of Cape Town tourism's newest hot spots—the Cape Malay Quarter, known as the Bo-Kaap ("above the cape") among the locals.

With sightseeing in South Africa growing rapidly after decades in which the country was boycotted for its racial-exclusion policies, Bo–Kapp residents are struggling to adapt to the sudden intrusion of visitors who come to experience "true South African life." But some veterans of the decades-long struggle for racial equality have begun to use the influx as a means of activism.

"We are the goodwill ambassadors of our country," says tour guide Mervin Wessels, a former student activist and high school geography teacher who turned to tourism several years ago as a way of educating people to the changes in his country since the end of apartheid in 1994.

He is not alone. Many tour guides are beginning to emphasize South Africa not as just a habitat for "big five" animals and exotic plants, but as a complex nation in the midst of an exciting transition toward multicultural democracy.

*Many tour guides are beginning to emphasize South Africa not as just a habitat for 'big five' animals and exotic plants, but as a complex nation in the midst of an exciting transition toward multicultural democracy.*

"It is important for a group to know that there are different people in different places of South Africa," says Bo-Kaap resident and former anti-apartheid campaigner Shereen Habib. The owner of Tanu Baru Tours, Habib has made a business of simply telling her story to visitors.

"I would like people to understand that South Africa, especially Cape Town, is a community of diverse backgrounds," she says.

Shortly after his release from prison in 1990, Nelson Mandela approached Habib to do her part for South Africa. While others channeled their political beliefs into government action or policy reforms, Mandela asked Habib to bring tourists back to South Africa. "He actually wanted me to put the area on the map," she says. "He said to me, 'You are my girl; you have to show off this area to the rest of the world.'"

For Wessels, the decision was both personal and political. Because most of South Africa's prime attractions were closed to people of color throughout the apartheid era, tourism had long been for whites only. When the opportunity arose for black South Africans to enter the field, Wessels says he jumped at the opportunity. Today, with a university education in African Studies, he knows his geography, history, and economics, but he also uses his own experience to connect with visitors.

As a South African talking about his life, he is able to bring visitors off the beaten path of other tours. At the same time, as a local, he is sensitive to community feelings and says he tries to align tourism with the development of township areas without exploiting the people.

When South Africa first faced an influx of visitors eager to see places they knew only from sensational headlines during the apartheid era, some guides were greeted with hostility. "It was becoming a zoo," says Wessels, recounting tales of German and Japanese tourists snapping pictures at all-black townships and impoverished squatter camps from behind the thick glass windows of luxury buses. Now, he encourages visitors to get out, walk around and use their cameras more discretely, as he introduces them to local residents.

Habib, too, says she tries to use tourism to help her community, not just put it on display. She has trained residents of the Malay Quarter to be tour guides, and has worked to convince local businesses of the importance of bringing visitors to the area.

Nevertheless, Habib is humble about her role.

"I can't speak about tourism and say it was my little thing, and I went about my little way—it wasn't that. It was an inclusive community effort," she says, adding that her first reaction to Mandela's request to get involved was, "Oh, no! What has he done to me?"

Almost immediately, Tana Baru Tours was thrown into the spotlight as it hosted a series of high-profile government guests, she says. In her view, it is important for companies and dignitaries to feel welcome in the community, so she trained residents to take the lead in guiding the VIP visitors.

Today, Habib's business is based on personal warmth. She invites visitors inside her home to share a meal or tea in her cozy living room. She also guides groups through the Cape Malay Quarter, making stops to show off the Bo–Kaap Museum, her mother's restaurant and her sister's coffee shop.

"I just want to show the area off as what it was," she says.

She also opens the door onto herself, telling her guests what life was like during apartheid, about her relationship with Mandela, about her brief foray into electoral politics in 1994 when she ran for office in the country's first democratic elections under the banner of the African National Congress (ANC).

Habib speaks about hiding refugees in her home at great risk to her life and liberty. If she'd been caught, she could have spent years in prison. Her most revered story is of her forbidden first marriage to a white man. Based on the separation of the apartheid regime, the two were not allowed to live together. Escaping to France, the two were strained by the difficulties of wanting to be together, to be in South Africa and not be arrested.

"The more you talk about things, the more you heal," Habib says. "South Africa went through a very quick healing process. There was just not time—we had to take charge."

For his part, Wessels includes tour stops at local craft centers where nongovernmental organizations (NGOs) sell beadwork, weavings, and other hand-made products to generate income for poor women.

One such stop is the Saartjie Baartman Community Center in Athlone, a mainly "colored" community—the term South Africans use for people of mixed race—just north of Cape Town. An NGO founded to support victims of domestic violence, the center serves as an umbrella for community-based organizations like Sonke, a group that trains abused women to make and sell goods for tourists as well as to lead tours.

Wessels says he recoils from the tendency of some visitors to come to Cape Town for one to two days, spending half of it atop the spectacularly beautiful Table Mountain plateau from where they look down on the city's three million inhabitants from a height of 3,500 feet. Or they visit theme parks where plastic houses simulate what it is like in Africa.

"I want to take them to the real McCoy," he says—and Khayelitsha is as real as it gets.

The sprawling township, more than twenty miles outside Cape Town, was established in 1984 to house black families forcibly removed from black neighborhoods and squatter camps near the city center. Today, its population tops one million. In the middle of it is Vicky's Bed and

Breakfast, set up by Vicky Ntozini and her husband Piksteel in the mid-1990s to capitalize on its authentic reflection of black life in the altered atmosphere of post-apartheid South Africa.

"Since the democratic elections here in 1994, there are many more tourists who come to South Africa, but most of them stay in the predominantly 'white' areas of the cities or in the carefully managed environment of the game parks," says Ntozini on her new Web site (journey.digital-space.net/vicky0.html). "By staying away from the townships, they miss learning about how most South Africans actually live."

Ntozini built the business out of her three-bedroom, scrap-iron-and-wood shack. This is her way of exposing visitors to the "real" South Africa, says Wessels, who has been bringing visitors to see her unique, no-star hotel for years.

In the beginning, neighbors jealous of the attention she received—and the income—had negative reactions, he says. But after Ntozini explained what she was trying to do, the community quickly backed her. Today, they are protective of the little business.

"There is an emerging market here," says Wessels. "The paradigm shift in tourism has been toward a more cultural experience."

"It is important that we get a holistic view of what is South Africa and what is Cape Town," he says. "We need to make you realize that you haven't seen it all—that you need to come a second time."

# Rebuilding the Nation

# Class Collision

By Darline Tunis
Soweto, South Africa

Winding driveways approach two-car garages under body-length windows leading to verandas. The homes, standing tall and statuesque, are surrounded by intricately designed gates and brick walls, and the lawns are as immaculate as the homes themselves.

In the Diepkloof Extension of Soweto, the largest and oldest black township in South Africa, houses for the emerging black middle class sell for up to R2 million ($350,000).

Five minutes away, brightly colored trash sprinkles the sidewalks and roads. Burning charcoal fills one's lungs, and thick black smoke fills the sky. This is also Soweto, where rows of small, brick, tin-roofed dormitories, known as hostels, are filled to overflowing with thousands of men, women and children.

Across the street, a bustling marketplace thrives. A bright pink billboard screams, "Love life, get attitude."

Another five minutes down the road lies Orlando West, the "Beverly Hills" of Soweto. This is the site of Winnie Mandela's sprawling brown and white mansion. It is also the neighborhood where Nelson Mandela and Archbishop Desmond Tutu formerly lived.

Although South Africa is often characterized as a "third world" country, the first and third worlds often reside here within just miles of each other.

> "We spend most of our time standing on the corner, smoking or watching TV. When we get tired, we have sex."

The distribution of income and wealth in South Africa is among the most unequal in the world, according to a report by Julian May, of Poverty and Inequality in South Africa. This inequality is readily apparent in housing.

In Camps Bay, a white, upper middle class suburb of Cape Town, houses valued up to R8 million ($1.4 million) are carved into the mountains and etched into the oceanside. These two- and three-story homes have large arching windows from which owners can view scenery that includes large boulders, sand, a blue green sea and the Twelve Apostles Mountains.

"Camps Bay is one of the most popular and most expensive suburbs in Cape Town," claims South Africa Online Travel Guide (www.southafrica-travel.net). It is THE place for chic urban beach life, with its restaurant, bar and café-filled promenade.

Over the mountain from Camps Bay, shortly after exiting the N2, one of the country's main transport arteries, visitors are greeted by millions of shacks. Made of tin, cardboard, plastic, wood, tarp and scraps, they huddle together for miles, dangerously lining unfenced train tracks. Among them are hair salons advertising Dark & Lovely products, telephone stations, meat markets and numerous residential homes.

Welcome to Khayelitsha, a black township established in Cape Town in the early 1980s.

The unofficial dirt roads of Khayelitsha are not wide enough for cars, and there is no room for gardens. Sanitation pipes do not work, and when it rains or snows, water seeps through the walls and breath can be seen. There is no basic sewage system.

Khayelitsha is nineteen miles from Camps Bay, yet the distinction between the poor township and rich suburb are familiar to Mandla Majola, one of over 500,000 blacks residing in Khayelitsha.

"In Camps Bay they go to the movies and to the waterfront to buy jackets and drive cars. In Khayelitsha there are no cinemas; we are struggling to buy bread," says the thirty-three-year-old activist, who devotes much of his time to educating his community on HIV/AIDS issues.

"There are no playing facilities in Khayelitsha," says Mandla. "We spend most of our time standing on the corner, smoking or watching TV. When we get tired, we have sex." Mandla recalls visiting a home in Camps Bay in which there were thirteen faucets. In Khayelitsha there is one tap for five hundred people.

On the other side of the N2 is Driftsands, a suburban community with asphalt roads wide enough for two cars going in opposite directions. Colorful, multi-story homes line the spacious streets, surrounded by immaculate lawns and locked gates.

The apartheid government claimed it did not intend for Khayelitsha to become a poor, overcrowded township for blacks. According to official pronouncements, the township was to be a solution to the mass migration begun at the end of influx control laws, but, instead it became a dumping ground for black families displaced from squatter settlements closer to Cape Town and a magnet for black families streaming in from the impoverished countryside.

"Up to ten thousand fathers, mothers, grandparents and children migrated every day to what was thought to be the land of milk and honey," says tour guide Mervin Wessels.

At first, government officials laid out a grid for lights, roads, electricity and water and offered blacks a plot of land for a numbered shack that was supposed to evolve into a home within five years. Instead, many poor families rented out what free space they had as a means of income, and the settlement quickly became severely overcrowded.

"Every available piece of remaining land was rented out," says Wessels. "After five years, instead of one shack per plot, there were ten shacks per plot." Soon the shacks were no longer counted.

The National Housing Project calls for the post-apartheid government to build one million houses every five years. In the eleven years since the African National Congress (ANC) was elected to run the country, 1.6 million houses have been built, but the demand keeps growing.

"One must accept it's still a drop in the ocean," says Wessels. "The rate of delivery has slowed down. They won't reach the one million-home goal in the next five years. They are losing their sense of urgency. It will be a challenge for any government to deliver."

Some activists warn that the population is becoming impatient. "Political leaders live in posh homes. We live in shacks. They haven't done anything for us," says Mandla, who understands that he now has a right to better housing. Without a fight, he is unlikely to get it, but he concedes that it is not easy to mobilize others to this fight.

Under the apartheid regime, anyone who fought for basic rights was subject to harassment, imprisonment or even death. Many who suffered the outrages and indignities of apartheid hesitated to take such risks, convinced that the chances of winning them were slim.

"I was never politically involved," says Lawrence Clements, a former postman in District 6, a community that was demolished in the 1980s under the Group Areas Act. "We were taught to be obedient to our teachers and our government. I just did my job and went home."

Today, however, with the political victory over apartheid behind them, many poor, black South Africans are losing patience with the slow pace of economic development—especially housing.

"We are tired of these shacks," says Mandla. "We have a right to better homes."

# HOUSING PROJECT OFFERS NEW HOPE

## BY EVAN KUHLMAN
### KHAYELITSHA, SOUTH AFRICA

Rose Maso maneuvers slowly through the corridor of her tidy, four-room brick house. Carefully hung lace curtains decorate the windows. The linoleum floor is swept clean.

Her plump fingers gingerly pat the freshly painted walls. Hints of brick peek out from the partially-completed ceiling. "This is my house," she boasts, raising her hand across her heart.

But the house is more than just her home—it is her creation.

Looking at her, it is difficult to imagine a hard hat in the place of her yellow felt hat, yet Maso is a trained bricklayer, and this house is the product of her hard work and physical skill.

There are no male craftsmen wielding hammers here. All the houses in the Victoria Mxenge project—named for a prominent anti-apartheid activist who was assassinated in 1985—have been built piece by piece by women. Like Maso, the other women—mostly single or widowed heads-of-household who are members of the Homeless People's Federation—have taken it into their own hands to provide homes for their families.

This community in the heart of South Africa's third largest black township was one of the organization's first housing projects. Affiliated with Shack Dwellers International (which it helped launch a decade ago), the

*We were trying to demonstrate that the poorest of the poor can still survive. Land ownership helps protect women from domestic violence, too.*

Homeless People's Federation was founded in 1991 by Patricia Matolengwe with thirty other women after she was forcibly moved by the apartheid government to Site B in Khayelitsha. Today, it boasts nearly 100,000 members throughout South Africa, ninety percent of whom are women.

In the sea of tin shacks that populate Khayelitsha, the organization is putting the meaning "New Home," as the township's name translates, to the test.

Nearly one-third of greater Cape Town's population of three million now lives in slums or squatter camps. Since the end of South Africa's apartheid-era "border control," during "which blacks were stripped of their citizenship and forced to carry passbooks authorizing travel outside designated tribal "homelands", ten thousand people a month have flooded into densely-packed informal settlements here. The result is miles and miles of new makeshift shacks.

Housing has been at the top of the priority list for the current government since the end of apartheid rule, but the mushrooming demand continues to far outstrip supply. When the African National Congress (ANC) took over with the election of Nelson Mandela in 1994, it promised to build a million houses every five years. Ten years later, many South Africans are skeptical that the next five-year mark will be met, as they are still waiting for housing.

"We were living in shacks, shacks that were burning and leaking when it rained," says Maso, whose home is surrounded by a sea of tin roofs that provide a constant reminder of the mass poverty that threatens to engulf her new community. However, the Victoria Mxenge project's success also inspires its members to do more.

The Homeless People's Federation is training women to be electricians, architects, and surveyors. With these skills, they have been able to train others, as well as take their talents into the workforce.

"We were trying to demonstrate that the poorest of the poor can still survive," says Matolengwe, who adds that land ownership helps protect women from domestic violence, too.

Women head the family in the majority of these households now, she says. When their houses are built, both their husband's and their names are put on the deed. According to Matolengwe, this helps secure a woman's safety because if she wants to kick out an abusive husband, she does not have to fear losing her home when her name is on the deed.

"We as women, let us try to feel the power as head-of-house, and let them feel the role of spouse," says Matolengwe.

But it has been a long road for women who started with no experience of any kind in home construction to get to this point. "We didn't even know how to do the measurements," says Maso.

The Victoria Mxenge houses are built on 150-square-foot lots, but their size and design vary depending on available funds. Buildings cost between R12,000 and R15,000 ($1,800 to $2,300), say federation leaders, and the infrastructure alone takes an additional R6,300 (nearly $1,000). Most of the money comes from a community savings association, to which all federation members contribute, and from government subsidies, which peaked at R10 million ($1.7 million) in 1995, but which are now declining. Women who borrow from the federation's savings plan pay the money back at a one-percent interest rate.

With the last of the houses in the Victoria Mxenge project now finished, the new village spans six streets with 112 family groups. Children spill out of the crèche (a community day care center) and play games and sing songs on the paved roads and in front yards.

Some women still sell fruits and vegetables to passersby to supplement their income, but hawking tomatoes and cabbage is not the only way these families survive today. For many, building their own house opened a new door to the future as skilled workers with paying jobs.

"We want to be part and parcel of everything that is happening here," says Maso.

The group is also reaching out to other neighborhoods to help them develop themselves, and has become a model for the country's revival, even as its success has brought worldwide recognition, including a visit from President Bill and Hillary Clinton in 1998.

But complacency is not yet setting in. "There is still a challenge as long as there is still homelessness in the country," says Matolengwe.

# Nuns Rebuild a School— and a Society

By Lyly Tran
Cape Town, South Africa

"The children burned down the school, but the parents were behind it," says Sister Lauda Libera. "They wanted to end apartheid, but they went about it the wrong way."

As she maneuvers her white Toyota Corolla from Cape Town's upscale Victoria and Alfred Waterfront Mall to Brooklyn, a poor neighborhood ten miles away where she teaches now, Sister Lauda describes her apartheid-era experience at the Magden School, where reform-minded teachers were squeezed between angry students and a government hostile to any loosening of race-based education policies.

She says the government was displeased, but took no action, when school administrators invited children of mixed race—categorized as "coloreds"—to the formerly all-white Catholic academy. But when they opened their doors to black students, she says, "They really clamped down on us."

The apartheid government forced the school to change its textbooks and its curriculum, and then took away its exams. In reaction, students burned the building down, leaving an already disadvantaged school with nothing, says Sister Lauda.

In this way the apartheid system not only violated the rights of individuals, it also crippled the ability of organizations like the Holy

*Tall and slight with shaggy gray bangs peeking thorough her veil, Sister Agatha Byrne surveys a well-decorated kindergarten classroom where most of the children sit in a circle awaiting story-time.*

Cross Sisters to meet their educational objectives, according to Sister Lauda. Many students refused to go to schools thus emasculated. As a result, many from that generation—now in their thirtys—never passed the sixth grade standard.

Today, the post-apartheid government provides partial funding to independent schools such as those of the Holy Cross Sisters. And Sister Lauda has not let up in her dedication to use education as a means to achieve greater social equality.

Though her high nose, large eyes and name indicate an Italian heritage, Sister Lauda is a native of Johannesburg. Ironically, her parents fled Europe to escape political turmoil there. At twenty-one, she entered the Holy Cross order because it was committed to educating the underprivileged.

Sixty years later, after enduring the destruction of the first school in which she taught, she works at the Holy Cross Family School in a black township east of Cape Town. There, the nuns and staff work to undo the segregation of apartheid by admitting students of all races, and providing them all with a good quality education.

Upon arriving, Sister Lauda rushes off to finish grading her students' work and turns her guide duties over to a colleague.

Tall and slight with shaggy gray bangs peeking thorough her veil, Sister Agatha Byrne surveys a well-decorated kindergarten classroom where most of the children sit in a circle awaiting story-time. A few stragglers in the back clean up some puzzles.

"Good morning, Sister Agatha," the students say in unison.

The younger children are in street clothes, unlike the uniformed seniors. At their age, emblems of wealth and status do not yet play a role in how the children interact, so they do not yet need uniforms, says Sister Agatha.

A thin, middle-aged black woman who identifies herself only as Ethyl also sits at one of the desks. She is a housekeeper at the school who is also training to be a teaching assistant, thanks to a program the school runs to upgrade the skills of their workers, and to help them gain the freedom to live where they want and to find better jobs.

In a fourth grade classroom, students color in "Proudly Made in South Africa" seals. "Why should you buy things that are made in South Africa and not somewhere else?" Sister Agatha asks.

"So that people can have jobs," one boy says.

She praises him.

Products made with resources and labor from South Africa are granted the "Proudly Made in South Africa" seal, part of a campaign started in 2001 to keep badly needed foreign exchange in the country. Shortly after the birth of the program, ninety two percent of South African consumers said they were willing to support companies with the certification in a survey conducted by the National Economic Development and Labor Council (NEDLAC), a joint initiative of government, business, labor and community groups.

In the hallway, Sister Agatha stops a young boy–who looks to be in third grade–as he leaves a classroom to ask why he is not wearing his jacket.

He misplaced it, he says.

You must have it somewhere, she tells him. "You're too rich to not have one."

Afterward, she remarks that some students are extremely well-off, and their parents can afford to feed them well and vacation in Europe and America. Other students, she says, are desperately poor. The mandatory uniforms for students beyond kindergarten help to conceal these disparities.

Every Monday a group of Holy Cross sisters goes to the local Pic-and-Pay to buy groceries to discreetly send home to poor families. The school also supports the long-term wellbeing of students by teaching them basic economics and management, starting in the first grade. Sister Agatha says she hopes that many can become vendors when they graduate.

The students practice salesmanship at the school's annual Christmas Bazaar. They must make what they sell, not buy it—including such items as fudge, painted pinecones and gift bags. To secure a table, the students pay R2 (30¢). Here, they learn to price items effectively, says Sister Agatha. After the fair, they pay a two percent commission to the school as form of income tax.

Even the archbishop of Cape Town visits this famous market, she says, laughing tenderly at the thought of her school-bred mini-merchants. The youngest ones, she says, often need extra time to figure out the math and have not yet grasped the art of bargaining, but many get a little help from their families.

"The parents are so supportive," says Sister Agatha, noting that it is not only the government that has changed since apartheid ended.

# CONFRONTING
# DOMESTIC VIOLENCE

# The Specter of Domestic Violence

## By Gina Patterson
## Cape Town, South Africa

One woman dies because of domestic violence every six hours in South Africa.

One in two women is in an abusive domestic situation.

Based on these and other statistics, South Africa leads the world in cases of domestic violence.

This is the message that reaches thousands of South Africans on prime time TV when they tune into "Family Ties," a documentary series that explores important social issues. This week the topic is domestic violence.

As the program opens, viewers see brick houses lining the street. Children play singing games; occasionally adults call out for them to come inside.

Suddenly, the camera zooms in on a sobbing Sophie Simabuhi, as streams of tears run down her wrinkled brown face. Her great-grandson struggles to wipe them away from her trembling lips as she tells her story.

On a quiet night in 2000, Simabuhi's daughter and granddaughter were killed—both at the hands of her granddaughter's angry boyfriend, she says. Her great-grandson witnessed the ordeal.

Tears roll slowly down the boy's face as he recalls the good times with his mother. He was just five years old when she was killed.

> *Finally, his growing frustration over not being able to provide for his family explodes into uncontrollable anger and violence.*

His forehead crinkles, and he looks down as he speaks about his life now—how he helps his great-grandmother walk.

"I have nothing," Simabuhi says quietly.

Without her daughter and granddaughter, she has no steady income, as they were the breadwinners. "I cannot work," she adds, turning to her great grandson. "I am too old."

Simabuhi says she wonders about her great grandson's future. At age nine, there is a big question about what will happen to him if she passes away. Year by year has flown by since the incident, and she questions how much longer she can go on. But she can only can wait and see what the future holds.

As the credits roll, the "Family Ties" program ends with many unanswered questions, not only about the Simbuhi family, but also about the plight of abused women throughout the country.

In recent years, an ever-larger percentage of South African women has been abused in their homes, making this a leading social problem today, according to social workers at the Sartjie Baartman Center, an umbrella agency for community groups dealing with violence against women and children. In some cases, families are torn apart; in others, the abuse is fatal.

For this reason the issue is now showing up in many cultural venues as artists and activists work together to get fellow South Africans to face this long-hidden problem.

The popular play "Shattered Dreams," recently performed at Johannesburg's renowned Market Theatre, demonstrates the tragic turn of events for a family after the husband loses his job and the wife is left to provide for them and their precocious teenage daughter.

Months go by and the husband still is not able to find work. Finally, his growing frustration over not being able to provide for his family explodes into uncontrollable anger and violence. First, he becomes emotionally abusive, tearing the family apart day by day until his distraught daughter commits suicide. When the father sees what has happened, he kills his wife and then himself.

Officials at the Sartjie Baartman Center say this scene is all too typical, and that society has a long way to go to deal effectively with such problems.

Although South Africa has strong new laws that identify domestic violence as a serious crime, the police often don't respond to women's calls, says Baartman Center director Ilse Ahrends.

Not enough people are trained to handle the problem, she adds. Many still think it's nobody's business to report the violence when it happens.

# Confronting a Culture
## of Abuse

By Renee Frojo
Cape Town, South Africa

After two months in the shelter, she has no home, no money, and two children to feed. Her ragged white T-shirt and faded blue pants hang off her frail figure as she paces barefoot on the gray-tiled lobby of the shelter.

She moves about in front of a wall of painted T-shirts adorned with phrases like "Why, Dad? Why?" and "When your girlfriend says no, she means no." The collage, created by former shelter residents, seems to voice her innermost thoughts.

"It's like it scars you for life, you know?" she says, as her seven-year-old son, Tom, runs in crying.

"I don't feel well," says the pale-faced boy, gazing at his mother whose tired expression gives her the appearance of someone well beyond her twenty-eight years.

For most of her life, Mandy Labusenagne has been a victim of domestic violence. After her last abusive relationship with a violent boyfriend, she sought refuge at the Saartjie Baartman Center for Women and Children.

The shelter offered her a temporary escape, but because more than 200 women come for help every month, there is a two-month time limit, regardless of the circumstances.

Now Mandy and her two children must once again return to their community and,

> *With her bags packed and things collected, she says that all she can do is wait and hope that things will be different*

along with tens of thousands of other destitute South African women, risk renewed domestic abuse and sexual violence.

With her bags packed and things collected, she says that all she can do is wait and hope that things will be different.

Threats to masculine identity from a stagnant economy that is undermining traditional male dominance within the family is a key factor in the rising levels of violence, according to many commentators. Women and children have become the most vulnerable targets.

Sexual violence against women is prevalent both in the home and on the streets, says Ilse Ahrends, an administrator at the Baartman Center. Child abuse is also increasing, with boys suffering mainly from physical assault, and girls becoming the victims of sexual aggression.

One in every four women is assaulted by her husband or partner every week, according to People Opposing Women Abuse (POWA), a nongovernmental organization (NGO) that researches gender-based violence. Because most abuse cases are unreported, the number is almost certainly much higher. POWA estimates that only one in twenty is reported to the police.

Women do not seek help because they are embarrassed, untrusting or afraid, but most of the time, they simply do not know their rights.

When Mandy arrived at the shelter three months ago with her two children, she was covered with scars and bruises and so desperate that she no longer feared to confide in someone and seek out help.

Mandy lived her entire life in Outter, a rural Afrikaner community near Cape Town. She and her two sisters were sexually abused by their father from the age of eight. She jumped into another abusive relationship with a boyfriend shortly after she left home looking for someone and somewhere to feel safe. She went on to endure emotional, physical, and economic abuse for the next five years, from the very beginning of this relationship.

"I wasn't allowed to work, or have friends, or even go out on my own," Mandy says. "I just had to keep myself distracted with the children and housework."

Mandy's experience is indicative of most cases of domestic violence in South Africa, say social workers here, but husbands and boyfriends are not the only abusers. Many times it is a family member like a father, a brother, or an uncle who abuses women who are close to them.

Victims of abuse tend to come from rural communities or townships, says Ahrends. Often, the violence takes place on the streets of their communities, where there are not enough shelters to support the vast number of women seeking help.

In Khayelitsha, a township next to Outter, nearly one million people live in one- and two-room shacks built nearly on top of each other.

Here, at least sixty cases of women and child abuse are reported every month, according to Mandla Majola, a spokesperson for the Treatment Action Campaign (TAC), which does education and advocacy work on HIV/AIDS within the community.

"Those who are raped usually are raped by someone they know, many times by a relative," says Majola. "They would rather sit down and talk about it with someone than report the case to the police."

One positive development is that domestic abuse, long shielded from public discussion by traditional mores that accepted it as "normal," is starting to be reflected in contemporary culture.

On a small stage in the theater district of Johannesburg, South Africa's largest city, the play "Shattered Dreams" narrates the experience of a family that disintegrates when the father loses his job. Unemployment makes him feel as if he has lost the status of the "head of the household," a feeling that is heightened as his wife struggles to bring in enough income to keep the family afloat.

Unable to find a job and threatened by his wife's success, he becomes insane with rage. For months, he verbally and emotionally abuses his family. Then, after driving his daughter to suicide, he kills his wife and shoots himself.

But contemporary culture is not the only place where the rising rates of violence against women have come to public awareness. The post-apartheid government is also responding to it at the highest levels, pushed in part by grassroots social movements like the TAC and POWA, and by increasingly active new women's organizations.

In 1998, Parliament passed a Domestic Violence Act that ensured protection against physical, emotional, or economic abuse, according to Connie September, a Member of Parliament from the ruling African National Congress (ANC). However, on a working level these protections have been hard to implement.

"We have a very good act on the books," says Ahrends. "But along with that needs to go training."

According to Ahrends, the police don't always respond well to cases of domestic violence. By not telling women their rights or assisting them in finding a shelter, they are not helping at all, she says.

"What really needs to change is the whole mind set of the society," Ahrends says. "Unless police and court officials are trained, it's going to be a slow process."

For her part, MP Connie September says the government needs to tackle legislation and make sure the services get to the women who need them: "I am certainly alive to the fact that we have very progressive policies in parliament, but many are not seen in real life."

Like Ahrends, September believes the real challenge lies in making women aware of and pushing them to demand access to these rights.

Meanwhile, several measures are being taken to send messages of understanding and awareness throughout communities. Along with demonstrations and posters, grassroots organizations are circulating informational materials that outline women's rights.

"They are not victims," says one booklet, titled It's an Order! A Simple Guide to Your Rights. "They are skillful survivors against tremendous odds. Their actions show their courage and their strength to survive."

Mandy's experience demonstrates that the message is getting through. Once she became aware of her rights, she filed charges against both her father and ex-boyfriend. Her father is now confined to thirty years in prison, though her boyfriend managed to escape.

"I don't know where he is," says Mandy. "And I don't even care, because I never want to see him again. He is in my past."

# PLAYING THE FIELD: RACE & GENDER IN THE NEW SOUTH AFRICA

BY JUSTINE DELUCA
JOHANNESBURG, SOUTH AFRICA

Melissa Sonnekus's bare feet silently glide across the floor as she walks to the back of the Boeing 747-400, midway between London and Johannesburg, to stand and stretch her legs.

Her shorts come down to the middle of her shins. She wears the same green uniform as twenty-two of her traveling companions, radiating pride in her membership on South Africa's national women's rugby team. Melissa, a white Afrikaner, says five weeks away from home is too long and claims that she has forgotten what South Africa looks like.

Several days later, Mpho Moagi, a black South African, sits at a round table in a posh Johannesburg hotel with three other female journalists—white, black and mixed race. Her hair is straightened and makeup neatly done. She wears a red blouse under a blue jacket.

Alive with passion, her hands accent each of her words as she speaks. When the other women take turns commenting and answering questions, she sits with her hands neatly folded and takes sips from a glass of water.

Both Melissa and Mpho have broken into fields that were once occupied solely by men, and which remain dominated by them today, at least at the top. Both are proud of themselves and their newly- transformed nation's achievements.

The end of apartheid opened new doors though which both women eagerly walked.

> *The mouth guard doesn't really work,"* she says, *pointing out that her two front teeth are loose from her moments of glory on the field.*

Now they face the arduous task of earning the respect and admiration that had previously been reserved by the government for white males, and working their way up in fields where glass ceilings still protect male decision-makers.

Melissa grew up watching her brothers play rugby from the sidelines. Until five years ago, women were only allowed to play rugby at home or on the beaches. Playing was forbidden to girls in South African schools or on any organized team.

In 1981, the South African Rugby Football Union (SARFU) was banned from international competition due to the government's apartheid-era policy of allowing only white players on the field. In 1990, after decades of protest and resistance, the government, still under white control but negotiating a transition to majority rule, began the process of reconciliation. As a result, South Africa's newly interracial rugby team was readmitted into the international arena—but women were still prohibited from playing.

Ten years later, SARFU announced that it would accept women's rugby into the union, too. On August 9, 2001, the SARFU Women's Rugby Program was officially launched at Loftus Versfeld in Pretoria, and female rugby players were given the opportunity to make their mark in sports history. Melissa was one of the twenty-two women chosen during practice games in Wales.

Though Melissa may have dreamed of playing rugby like the boys as she grew up, Mpho never imagined that one day she would be a journalist. She always thought she would become a teacher or take work in a field typical for women. In this respect, she is part of a growing new phenom-enon—women taking entry-level positions in formerly all-male professions as the society moves toward greater equality in more than just racial terms.

The South African parliament is increasing the diversity of the country's workforce through a policy of affirmative action—termed black empowerment here, but also aimed at gender discrimination—which was passed in 1998.

Nevertheless, according to Afrikaner journalist Cornia Pretorius, race, not gender, is still the dominant criterion for affirmative action. Pretorius adds that regardless of how many women are now entering formerly closed professions, most decision-making power remains in the hands of men.

Pretorius says that promotion may increase a woman's salary and change her title, but this does not mean she will gain power to determine the nature of the work itself. "Women can only climb so high before reach-ing the ceiling," she says.

For her part, Mpho says she fell into journalism, but once there she sought to become a voice for those who were not positioned to express their needs.

Drawing upon her own experiences, she tries to shed light on issues that deserve more exposure.

However, each piece Mpho works on is scrutinized by her male editor. She says it has been difficult to obtain permission to investigate and research topics such as abortion and rape. Although such issues affect a large number of people, they are not readily accepted by her editor.

Mpho attributes her editor's lack of interest to fear. She says that male responses are often used as a counter-balance to her woman-oriented initiatives. "What a man's reaction to a piece will be is at the forefront of the editor's mind," she says, adding that the important thing is to enlighten those who are ignorant of social issues and rights.

Women journalists are stereotyped as writing from the heart, she says. Media pieces are divided into two categories: soft and hard. Articles that Mpho produces are often classified as soft because they deal with issues that are considered more feminine.

Women are criticized because they "work from the heart and not the brain," she says. But many women do not see this as a detriment. Melissa Sonnekus is one of them.

As she describes her experience as a woman rugby player, she touches the springbok embroidered on the left side of her jersey with her hand and pats it twice. The 'jumping antelope' is the emblem used by both the male and female rugby teams.

She also wears a silver medallion around her neck, a gift from a friend back home. She has to take all her jewelry off before donning the shoulder, chest and headgear.

Melissa says the feeling of wearing the patch upon her chest and standing in front of the crowd singing the national anthem before the start of each game is amazing. She stares into the distance as the memories fill her mind, smiles, and then nods her head with satisfaction.

The South African women's rugby team trains all year round. "It is impossible to take a month off," says Melissa, who points out that the British women's team has been playing for about thirty years, and their skills show that.

In the last match the U.K. team gave them "a bit of an ass whooping," but Melissa says she and her team remain confident in their abilities. The match was only lost by one point, she adds—"not a convincing lead."

She says that her flight is paid for, but that the women do not earn a living from their play. All have day jobs—Melissa is an industrial psychologist—and rugby doesn't put a coin in their pockets. Instead, they play for pride.

Although Melissa works throughout the week, every Saturday she plays in a rugby game. Each provincial team competes with the others, until two teams are identified from the north and the south to battle for the national trophy.

Meanwhile, there are costs to the players not measured in money. The mouth guard "doesn't really work," she says, pointing out that her two front teeth are loose from her moments of glory on the field.

Although these committed women play with strength, speed, and skill, the media are slow to recognize their determination. According to former journalist and now media studies professor Anton Harber, women's sports are not considered as interesting or important to the media as men's.

Mpho says that what has helped her endure a male-dominated profession is her chance to dream and hope. She wants to give a voice to people and expose corruption. Journalism allows her to go somewhere and investigate, to expose and to show people that there are options other than their current state of affairs.

Perhaps someday she will write a feature on a woman like Melissa that male rugby fans will read, too.

# MEN DOMINATE WOMEN TO DEFINE SELF-WORTH, SAY RESEARCHERS

### By Katie McCarthy
### Johannesburg, South Africa

"They believe that men cannot be men without violence," says Detlev Krige, a doctoral candidate in anthropology at South Africa's prestigious University of the Witwatersrand.

The young men whom he interviewed in the black township of Soweto would rather hold a woman down than let her make more money than they do, he says. They feel imprisoned by their masculinity.

"When addressing the issue of women in South Africa, you cannot talk about gender without talking about men," he says, adding that he wants to help empower women, but he knows it cannot happen without examining and changing the mindset of men.

Krige says that these young men are from similar backgrounds. Their parents were poor, and they are stuck at the same level of poverty. However, some of their peers have moved on and are doing better. Suddenly, they are not in the same league as their former friends, and they see themselves as not achieving much.

The luxuries enjoyed by most whites were not attainable for black South Africans during the apartheid era, no matter what they did. Now, though new opportunities are opening for blacks, it is hard for many of those who were born into poverty to take advantage of them, according to Krige, and this pushes them to find alternatives to enhance their status.

> *Staying home is hard for men who believe they must be the protector and provider, and few are prepared to do so.*

The young men believe that women get in relationships for security, homes and cars, and having money is now the dominant concern in hetero-sexual relationships. "The men feel helpless without money," Krige says.

Meanwhile, many South African men are finding their masculinity challenged by the empowerment of their wives. Often, each success a woman achieves leads a man to become less trusting and supportive.

There is also a lot of jealousy among both men and women, so it is tough to build a stable relationship. Even for those who try marriage, infidelity is common.

Many people insist that "as long as I don't see it, it's not there." Today these young men say that marriage is just a partnership to have kids.

Meanwhile, says Krige, they are caught in a squeeze. They come under pressure from friends in gangs who call them weak if they are not having more than one woman, while women are pushing them to be loyal and either get jobs—which are scarce—or stay home to care for their families.

But staying home is hard for men who believe they must be the protector and provider, and few are prepared to do so. Men need to feel they are the heads of their household, and do not easily take orders from female partners. During the anti-apartheid struggle they could assert their masculinity by confronting the government, even if they could not find work, but today they are at a loss.

Krige thinks that part of the problem is that the role models these men had when growing up never challenged gender roles. Instead of seeing common respect between parental figures, they often watched their mothers get humiliated. New models are needed.

One group trying to fill this gap is the Men's Forum, which promotes new ideas of masculinity at the community level. They are emphasizing protection in all aspects of sex to help protect men's health. They are also telling men to let women ask to use protection in sex, or even ask about infidelities, arguing that empowering women does not take away from their masculinity.

Nevertheless, many South African men are having a hard time finding their place between being the titular head of a household and being a supportive husband to a breadwinning wife, especially if they are not working themselves.

Krige says that men who are searching to find their role in this new society are often left asking themselves: What does it mean to be a father? And what does it mean to be a man?

# SAVING THE CHILDREN

# THE LOSS THAT WON'T GO AWAY:
## ONE WOMAN'S STORY

### BY FAY STAMBUK
### JOHANNESBURG, SOUTH AFRICA

"My son, my beautiful son, he is gone," cries Lebo as she wipes off the tears that roll down her embarrassed face with the palms of her hands. "After one week I came to pick him up, but he was gone."

The salty drops leave jaded traces, as the disco ball shamelessly projects its careless glitter around the room and throws shadows across her desolate face.

The Capitol, a small retro-style music café in the Rosebank section of Johannesburg, is her host this night. She is dressed in tight, white, stretchy jeans enhanced with neon ornaments, which glow with her rhythmical swinging to the powerful music. Her closely shaved head highlights her dangling earrings and their spontaneous flirtation with the melodies of the DJ's house remix.

Shortly before her tragic disclosure, she passes her hand across the doorway to another room briefly, waves, still smiling jauntily, and then turns on her heels and enters the "White Room."

Once inside, she sits on her knees, bouncing slightly up and down, right and left, on the bright white 70s-inspired sofa. Her red high heels move as she swings.

"Sorry for being a gate-crasher," she says.

She gives her name only as Lebo. She is twenty-five years old and lives in New Orleans, a neighborhood in Soweto, one of the oldest

> *She does not want to talk about it. Yet, as she catches her breath, the story begins to break through her self-imposed silence, as if it had a life of its own.*

and best-known "townships" in South Africa, set up in the 1930s to house black laborers separately from whites. She calls herself the proud mother of an eight-year old girl. She has another four-and-a-half-month-old son, but he is gone now.

As the conversation continues, her face goes into a dark, heavy shadow, silencing the liveliness that surrounded her just seconds ago.

"What happened to your son?" a listener asks.

Lebo shakes her head testily. She does not want to talk about it. Yet, as she catches her breath, the story begins to break through her self-imposed silence, as if it had a life of its own.

"I brought him to a crèche," she explains, as her eyes fill with water. "I didn't know what to do. I returned to pick him up, but then he was gone."

She pauses in order to discreetly brush off her tears.

A crèche in South Africa is what they call a daycare center—an initiative to support disadvantaged working women or to provide basic needs for children with sick parents, many of whom suffer from acute illnesses caused by the HIV/AIDS epidemic that is leaving a growing number of infants to grow up homeless orphans.

But, occasionally, tragic and incomprehensible disasters strike the children lucky enough to find themselves at these crèches. "Some children get stolen by infertile couples; others get abducted by community members," says one volunteer at the Limpho Hani Centre, a crèche in the Doornkop area of Soweto. "These people think they have the authority to punish mothers for their 'misbehaved' actions."

"These kinds of situations are difficult to quantify," says Dr. Sheila Meintjes, a university professor in nearby Johannesburg who actively supports the Doornkop crèche. "But a mother might bring a child one morning, interact with the staff, even pay a small fee, and then never return."

Abandonment and abduction are not common occurrences at the crèche, says Meintjes, though she admits she lacks exact numbers.

"But having said that, the problem of abandoned children has been around a long time in South Africa," she adds. "The hospitals are the ones left with the babies. Thus, it is worthwhile looking into the Department of Social Development."

The Pretoria-based Department of Social Development's mission is "to enable the poor, the vulnerable and the excluded within South African society to secure a better life for themselves, in partnership with them and with all those who are committed to building a caring society," according to the department's Web site (www.welfare.gov.za).

The department says it does this by formulating policies and legislation, as well as by drafting implementation strategies, but it, too, lacks precise statistics on abandoned children. Nevertheless, the ANC government's identification of this as a major social problem indicates that Lebo's loss is part of a larger pattern of domestic violence, substance abuse and economic distress afflicting the country's impoverished majority. Yet, for Lebo, the tragedy is hers alone to struggle to understand.

"I don't know—maybe I was careless," Lebo says.

"But I was out of it, like when you have a car crash. You don't remember where you are, who you are, what happened, why it happened," she says, with no evident control over her emotions. "But God knows what's in my heart. I don't care what people think."

The story becomes more and more muddled as she tells it, but her composure is so tense and bewildered that it allows no room for interference.

Only fifteen minutes after the initial jolly encounter, Lebo sits stiffly—and almost tamed—on the white sofa. Her eyes and face are dry, leaving no trace of the emotions she exposed minutes earlier. Only the coldness that veils her stare gives away her suppressed pain.

Her eyes pierce through the room towards the inside of the café as she catches sight of her male companion. She smiles as he approaches her. Like a master of deception, she bans the previous sorrow and takes her date's hand.

As he pulls her away impatiently, she escapes his restraint and whispers: "I love my son so much, so much, and I pray that God will give him back to me."

# Lebo Reluctantly Obeys—
# Like a Dog in the Park

By Justine DeLuca
Johannesburg, South Africa

The hip young black woman walks by smiling.

She dances with her knees bent towards each other, feeling the groove of the music as the bass thumps loudly behind her.

She works her way towards the floor in tight, painted pants that glow under the blue lights of the Capitol, a chic bar in Rosebank, a mixed-race, middle-class neighborhood complete with four-star hotels and a shopping mall, twenty minutes from downtown Johannesburg.

Her knees that once spread wide for the conception and birth of two children are clenched as she dances, a subtle signal that she is not as relaxed and casual as she seems.

When the song ends, she springs upon the white couch, smiling and laughing, as she describes herself to a stranger as a "gate crasher," delving into the world of others.

Identifying herself only as Lebo, she says she is intrigued by those who just sit and allow people to come to them, doing their own thing without a care to others. Her teeth shine brilliantly as her smiling face bubbles with excitement, accentuated by the loud music and her lilting Botswana accent.

Her words, like a waterfall, roll constantly from her lips, flowing from one topic to another while revealing selective scenes from her life and leaving little space for questions from listeners.

> She describes her experience as like being in a car crash, where at the end you or your friend is dead: "I wonder where he is. I wonder what he is doing right now."

She complains of having to buy new clothes to fit her dwindling figure, saying she cannot control her weight. She has been losing and losing, and cannot explain why.

Suddenly, Lebo blurts out that she is spending another night out, drinking to forget. She is happy to pose for a photo, and adjusts her breasts under a pink top that accentuates her cleavage. Afterward, she sits back down on the couch with her back straight and legs crossed, dangling her left foot in the air.

"I always sit to show my shoes match my shirt," she says, as she twirls her foot about in the stylish, strapped shoe. It is important to her to show the care that she takes in preparation for the world outside her door. She strives to look "normal"—which she is in more ways than she chooses at first to acknowledge.

More than half the women in South Africa are not economically active. Without monetary resources of their own, they often remain in abusive relationships and environments to survive. She is one of them.

Lebo is neither a student nor a worker. "I am a mom," she says and is silent for a few moments. The air becomes stiff. She looks hard through her dark brown eyes, searching for her words. Her youngest child is four-and-a half months old, she says, but she tries to avoid talking about him.

"Let's talk about happier things," she says.

After a few moments, she turns the conversation back to her son. She says she left her newborn at a crèche two months ago—the term South Africans use for childcare centers.

One week after Lebo left her son, she returned to take him home, but he was no longer there. She replays the moments before she left him off. She says she is ashamed.

Lately, her mother has been asking to see her grandson, but Lebo says she hasn't told her that he is lost.

She describes her experience as like being in a car crash, where at the end you or your friend is dead. "I wonder where he is. I wonder what he is doing right now," she says.

"I'm drinking to forget, so I get drunk," she adds, sounding like the loneliest woman in the world. But she has plenty of company in her plight.

Social worker Ilse Ahrends estimates that between thirty percent and fifty percent of the women who are admitted to the Saartjie Baartman Centre for abused women and children, which she directs, have been abusing alcohol.

Shelters such as this provide women with a safe haven and educate them about their legal rights. The facility is a temporary escape from abuse and violence, and it is always at maximum capacity.

Ahrends says they have to turn many women away, and that many more outlets are needed for South African women to cope with their turmoil.

But Lebo is not ready to take this step, and still chooses alcohol to deal with her pain.

"I lost him. Can you imagine laughing with your son for two and a half months?" she asks, as her hands and words fly through the air.

"I could have aborted," she says, striking her left hand across her right and gesturing down at her womb. "No shame in that."

But she says she chose to have her son: "I love my son."

Lebo says she was raised by her aunt. She says her mother did not show any support or care: "She was a drunk. She is my biological mother, but she was not there for me. She could be gone but not my son."

Lebo says she stays away from her own daughter so that she can "grow up straight."

She strikes one hand past the other and pushes away from her body.

Tears stream steadily down her face.

She wonders where he is now, what he looks like, what he is doing. She tries to imagine what the eyes that look upon her son are seeing. She systematically wipes tear after tear away.

"We used to laugh together," she says, as she struggles to maintain her breath, articulating precisely each word under her wet nose.

"Do you know what the name I gave him means?" she asks. "The name I gave him means present."

"Can you imagine?" she asks. "He used to laugh at me, and I should have known."

Lebo says she came to the Capitol club with a man. She scrunches her face in his direction. He buys her drinks and watches over her as she talks, but adds nothing himself.

"I love my son," she keeps repeating until the man signals to her that it is time to leave. Lebo reluctantly obeys—like a dog that is forced to leave her companions at the park.

# ONE WOMAN'S DREAM ENSURES CHILDREN'S FUTURE

By Evan Kuhlman

Dobsonville, South Africa

"This is the way we wash our face," the voices of children chime from within a small stucco building.

Entering the classroom, Nthabiseng Hlongwane gleams with pride. The children's small hands brush across their cheeks, their smiles illuminating the dark room.

A tiny boy clings to the older woman's leg, wrapping his arms and legs just above her bright orange tennis shoes. In one motion Hlongwane sweeps him onto her back and adjusts a beige towel to securely wrap him in.

Drawing on instinctive maternal interest, this grandmother figure has become a leader in a quiet childcare revolution in Doornkop, a squatter camp on the outskirts of South Africa's largest and oldest black township.

After arriving with three small children of her own, Hlongwane became concerned that no one in the squatter camp was looking after the children when they returned home from school, or while their parents were at work. Her concerns intensified when a small child was raped while her mother was away, she says.

South African mothers, many of whom lack husbands, have little choice in whether to work or to stay at home to raise their children. Childcare remains their responsibility on top of supporting their families financially. Thus, the crèche (what South Africans call a daycare center) is a relief.

> *Like the sprouting greens, the future of the crèche remains uncertain, but this does not stop Hlongwane from tending to the children in her care as if they were her own.*

In 1996, Hlongwane founded the Limpho Hani Centre to service the Doornkop community. After proposing a childcare facility, the people in the community informally allowed Hlongwane to begin clearing a space on part of an old garbage dump. Piece by piece, she began removing debris from the area.

Her workforce quickly grew.

For a cold drink and a cookie or a biscuit, the young boys in the area worked to create the new plot. With the help of University of the Witwatersrand professor Dr. Sheila Meintjes, the childcare center is developing into a permanent structure and school for the children. Meintjes organizes university student volunteers, helps secure financial aid, and solicits voluntary legal advice for the crèche.

Colorfully painted tires spring from the South African red soil and lead into the complex. Sporadically arranged play equipment hints at the presence of the center's children. The old slide glimmers in the sun, reflecting against the zinc buildings of the classroom and kitchen.

Seventy small faces look out of the room. Each day the children arrive early to be fed a warm breakfast. As the sun rises, the children scribble, draw, and paint.

When families can pay, the fee for care is R70 per month ($10). It is often hard for families to come up with the funds, as this leaves them with little to provide for school supplies and food for the children, but these fees are necessary, as they are the only source of income for Hlongwane.

Donations from international visitors and non-governmental organizations fill in the rest of the center's monetary needs, says Gillian Goodall. A retired schoolteacher, Goodall has partnered with Meintjes to help with the crèche's development.

Hlongwane houses a dozen children at her home, within walking distance from the crèche. Most of the girls and boys—many of whom are AIDS orphans—are not eligible for government subsidies, which require a valid birth certificate. Out of the twelve children, only two have the necessary paperwork.

"The community does not help her as much as Nthabiseng helps them," says Goodall.

In addition to running the crèche, Hlongwane helps unemployed mothers make crafts to sell for supplemental income. The center is also working to give formal training to four other women employed to tend to the children. These women have become vital to the future of the crèche since the death of Hlongwane's daughter.

As she speaks, Hlongwane adjusts knotted scarves around her head and neck, a symbol of mourning for her daughter. Only a couple of weeks previously, Sheila died at the age of twenty-four.

AIDS is the suspected cause of Sheila's death, though even until her passing she denied being infected both to her mother and to her doctors. Sheila's death has hurt the crèche both spiritually and financially, as she supported her mother's efforts.

While the crèche provides childcare for preschool aged children, Hlongwane also supplies meals for school-aged children, and has created a soccer league for some of the boys. In an effort to keep the children safe after school, she organized the Pho Youngstons team.

"First of all, I so wish to see these children [have] a better school, in a better building and to get better food for them," says Hlongwane.

Hlongwane is not a stranger to action—or bravery. During the early 1990s, she stood strong with other woman on the site of her home to protest the government bulldozing of the community's shacks. Hlongwane led a group of homeless women in stripping off their clothes, an action taken to symbolize the stripping of their rights, and to gain attention to their cause.

On less than R1.70 per child, Hlongwane provides three meals a day. Soup is made from vegetables grown in a modest garden behind the main building. Hlongwane tends greens and potatoes with the children. Kneeling between carefully tended rows, she harvests leaves from mysterious plants whose names are unknown to her because the seed packets are printed in German.

Like the sprouting greens, the future of the crèche remains uncertain, but this does not stop Hlongwane from tending to the children in her care as if they were her own.

# A Woman Builds a Better Life for her Children

## By Katie McCarthy
### Doornkop, South Africa

Nthabiseng Hlongwane is the biological mother of three, but today, as she reaches middle age, she calls twelve children her own.

When she originally arrived at this informal settlement—what South Africans call a squatter camp—she was a young single mother with no support. Her family began to expand exponentially in 1996 when she took in the orphans of her community, many of whose parents had died from AIDS.

To accommodate her growing brood, she searched for a daycare center or a preschool in the area, but found none. Lacking more than a bare subsistence income from unemployment, she had stark limits on what she could afford.

Unable to rent a house for her growing family, she improvised by cleaning up a public dumping ground on the outskirts of Soweto, Johannesburg's largest and oldest African township.

The squatter camps are areas where families set up temporary shacks while they wait for government housing. It took Hlongwane months to make the site livable, but she was finally given informal rights to the land after cleaning it up.

In 1998 she started a small vegetable garden on the reclaimed land. Today, it has grown enough to feed all the children of the crèche.

> *Hlongwane's relentless hope and struggle not only serve the children but also set an example for many women who are trying to make a positive difference in their lives and the lives of others.*

In the past year she has also hired unemployed builders in the area to put together the three structures that now make up the crèche.

The rectangular, one-story buildings are small, but clean. Wood-beamed ceilings show in one that is not yet finished but is slated to be a classroom. Another, already completed, has a working kitchen. All three are dimly lit and sparsely furnished but greatly appreciated by the children and their teachers.

Hlongwane says she came up with the idea for the crèche because many parents are gone for twelve-to-fifteen hours a day while searching for jobs to keep their families alive and fed. This left many children taking care of one another, even though they were very young. Older children often wandered the streets and got into trouble because they had no positive influences. Some turned to crime.

The crèche now cares for about seventy children. Of the nine Hlongwane adopted who were either abandoned here or are AIDS orphans, only two have achieved the legal status needed to receive government social grants, she says.

Hlongwane charges R70 per month for the care of each child, and she says she gets about half of this consistently. Parents pay when and what they can. The children are fed three meals at the crèche, and most stay there between six in the morning and six at night.

To aid in the building of the crèche, she has gotten local schools to come in and use it as a community service project, but the women in the community—mothers of the children—do little to help. Instead, she helps out the mothers. However, Hlongwane says the payments of these families are her only source of income.

Gill Goodall, a retired white teacher who helps at the crèche, says that Hlongwane's relentless hope and struggle not only serves the children but also sets an example for many women who are trying to make a positive difference in their lives and the lives of others.

Goodall has helped her apply for government funding. She says the Department of Health will give Hlongwane R1.50 a day (25 cents) for a destitute child. The process to apply is very difficult, however, and if she gets the grant, it will only last for three years.

Meanwhile, they are developing a formal curriculum, because the center is now more of a caring facility than a preschool. Goodall says they would like the curriculum to have a more solid work program. Currently, there is not enough space or resources to split up the classroom into age groups, so all children are grouped together, from toddlers to ages five or six.

During one hour, Hlongwane carries four different children on her back, treating every one as her own. When the visiting Simmons students leave, she gives each a big hug, and thanks them for taking an interest in her life.

With a toddler strapped on her back, she says: "I want to see my children have a better life and go to better schools."

# Overcoming Poverty in Africa—
# One Life at a Time

By Renee Frojo
Soweto, South Africa

Rubbing the sleep out of their half-opened eyes, the toddlers peeked their heads around the doorway before wandering barefoot onto the dirt floor outside. It was right after lunchtime, and some had just awakened from a midday nap. Wide smiles beamed from their dark round faces as they approached us.

After the first few came closer to get a better look, the rest grew more comfortable and followed suit, shrieking in excitement at our surprise visit. Attracted by the digital camera in my hand, one little boy hesitantly approached me.

As I looked down to take his picture, I could see my reflection in his deep brown eyes that were fixed on me like magnets. I followed him into the tiny schoolroom, where more than fifty more innocent eyes gazed up at us.

This was our second venture into Soweto, the oldest and largest "township" near Johannesburg, where blacks were forced to live during the era of racial separatism known as apartheid. I was traveling with a group of women students from Simmons College who were exploring women's roles in South Africa since the apartheid system was dismantled in the mid-1990s.

Through the tinted glass of our chartered tour bus, I gazed at miles of unpaved roads lined with small brick houses and unstable tin shacks. I had become familiar with the sight of

> *Children would wander the streets unattended and unfed. There were no shelters to provide a temporary home or protection. Some had been abandoned or their parents had died of AIDS.*

so much poverty from a distance, but it was not until we stepped off the bus to visit the small crèche—a daycare center—in Soweto's Doornkop neighborhood, that I got a close-up look.

On arrival, Gill Goodall, a retired teacher from a well-to-do white suburb who volunteers at the crèche, quickly briefed us on the history of the area and the establishment of the center.

According to Goodall, unemployment is still very high and the community of Doornkop remains in severe poverty. Left behind by a society in change, the fate of the community's children became the urgent concern of one of the township's most exceptional women, Nthabiseng Hlongwane.

After leading a movement to in the 1990s to establish Doornkop as an informal settlement, Hlongwane's focus was geared towards providing a shelter for the future generations of the community, said Goodall.

Children would wander the streets unattended and unfed. While their parents were at work or searching for jobs, there were no shelters to provide a temporary home or protection. Some of children had been either abandoned or their parents had died of AIDS.

"Nthabiseng was deeply concerned that no one was looking over the children, and something immediate had to be done," said Goodall.

Hlongwane was able to persuade the town council to grant her a piece of land to build a child-care center. Now known as the Limpho Hani Center, it caters to fifty-to-sixty preschool-aged children every day. From 6 a.m. until 6 p.m. the center is filled, seven days a week.

"I stay with them, look after them, and provide them with clothes," said Hlongwane, who cares for nine of the orphaned children in her own home.

Hlongwane said that when she founded the crèche it was a dump. She rounded up a group of young boys to help her clean up the area and easily bribed them into helping by rewarding them with food after a hard day's work.

"It took ages to clean, and we only received informal rights to the plot," said Goodall. "Right now they are still trying to get it formalized."

During my visit, the center appeared modestly bare. Only three buildings surrounded the dirt-floored quad, and only one zinc building served as the classroom. The other zinc building was the kitchen, in which volunteers helped prepare three meals a day for more than fifty children. It also served lunch to the hungry older siblings who passed by the crèche on their way home from school.

"I cook almost all the meals here," said Dismakatso Motau, a third-year politics student who volunteers at the crèche almost every afternoon. "It is a pleasure for me, especially when I can see how much they enjoy it."

Since the crèche is working on limited funding, the children were mainly fed soup from vegetables they gathered from a garden Hlongwane planted behind the school.

According to Goodall, the financial situation is dire. The center charges a fee of about $10 per month for any family who can afford it.

"It's still a huge work in progress," Goodall said. "Community involvement is crucial."

Some students helped out by making quilts and crocheting shoes for the children. There were also four teachers working, with no formal training, to teach English and help look after the children. The materials they use to teach with, such as paper and art supplies, were all from donations.

Inside the classroom, a few ragged posters painted with English words and pictures hung off the walls. On the floor lay a dirty and abandoned teddy bear with stuffing spilling out of its missing leg.

The school seems to be doing what it can with what it has. The children all appeared well groomed and well fed, but only a few could communicate with us in English.

"I wish to see these children at a better school and I want to see this place grow," Hlongwane said. "This is my dream, but it is just a dream."

# PHOTOGRAPHS

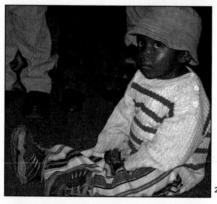

1. SABC-FM's Talia Sanhewe.
2 & 3. Limpho Hani
   crèche, Soweto
4. Downtown Soweto

Photos by Dan Connell
The Image Works

1. Tour guide Shereen Habib, Bo-Kap
2. T-shirts at Saartjie Baartman Centre
3. WISER gender researchers
4. FUNDA director Charles Nkosi

1. COSATU gender coordinator
   Mummy Jafta
2. Constitution Hill Museum
3 & 4. Constitutional Court

1. Bo-Kap, Cape Town's Malay quarter
2. Gina Patterson
3. Christine Franey
4 & 5. Formerly homeless woman with new house

1. SABC-FM's Talia Sanhewe
2. Fay Stambuk
3. Kate Lolley
4 & 5. Copper etchings at
   Constitutional Court

1. Mandela's work site at Robben Island prison
2. Artist Thuli Bhengu
3. WISER researcher Grace Khunou
4. Black women in business

1. Evan Kuhlman, Erin Rook, Fay Stambuk, Lyly Tran at TAC briefing
2 & 4. ANC MPs Connie September and Ncumisa Kondlo
3. Artist Nelsie Ndimande

1. Fay Stambuk, Justine Deluca, Renee Frojo, Evan Kuhlman, Lindsey Varney
2. Justine Deluca with artist Thuli Bhengu
3. Amanda Cary at TAC briefing
4. COSATU gender coordinator Mummy Jafta
5. Cape Point

1. Gentrification threatens Bo-Kap 's identity
2–4. Women's co-op, Khayelitsha

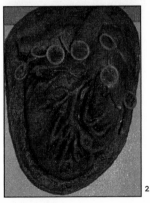

1. Hout Bay
2. Nelsie Ndimande depicts AIDS impact on S.A. heart
3. Darline Tunis & Gina Patterson
4. Robben Island view of Cape Town

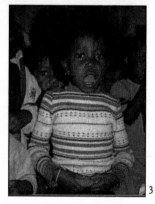

1 & 3. Limpho Hani
   crèche, Soweto
2. Alex Carithers
4. Katie McCarthy

1. Bo-Kap worker
2. Artist Lorraine Ndlovuheart
3. Tea in Bo-Kap
4. Constitution lesson for kids

# DEALING (OR NOT) WITH HIV/AIDS

# DEATH BY DENIAL

By Amanda Cary
Khayelitsha, South Africa

Zeldah waits eagerly for her turn.

The wooden benches in the small waiting room overflow with people. One woman sits motionless in a trance. Another sits calmly, as if she were on her living room couch watching a TV soap. Most just look exhausted.

Their wait could be up to three hours—on a good day.

Still, Zeldah, with her short spiky hair, looks as if she is on a mission. Finally, it is her turn. She plants herself on the cracked wooden bench as if she were giving an official press conference.

She smiles, relieved that her chance has finally come. She knows she may have to remain several more hours in the cramped waiting room before she actually sees a doctor, but she is not waiting just to be examined. She waits to tell her story.

The healthy-looking twenty-six-year-old speaks softly, but with conviction. Her baby got sick in 1997, she says calmly. Then he died.

Three years later, Zeldah discovered lesions on her own skin and in her mouth, and her hair began to feel like that of a baby.

Zeldah, like many others waiting here, is HIV-positive and has tuberculosis (TB). But she is intent on letting people know that she takes her medicine and is healthy now.

When she first tested positive for HIV, her CD4 count, a test of her immune cells, was

"You can't run away from it. It's like the pigment of your skin. You accept it."

fifteen. A normal CD4 count, indicating the health of one's immune system, is 500-1500. Her immune system was virtually non-existent, and she was fighting both TB and meningitis.

To treat the HIV, she was put on antiretroviral drugs (ARVs). She also took fluconazole to treat her thrush, an opportunistic infection of the mouth or throat, and was started on a TB treatment regiment. She is now healthy, and she wants everyone to know it.

"I know these ARVs are working," she says, as if testifying in court.

ARVs have been used successfully to treat HIV in America for several years now. But in a poor township outside of Cape Town, South Africa, Zeldah feels she needs to convince people.

Those seated around her listen and nod with enthusiasm. They are all awaiting treatment in a clinic run by Médecins Sans Frontières (MSF) in Khayelitsha, twenty miles outside Cape Town. Khayelitsha is a township of dirt roads and crowded shacks thrown together out of discarded wood, scraps of metal, torn plastic and other odds and ends. The highly unsanitary living conditions contribute to the high rates of HIV and TB.

Other factors that predispose people to infection—like poverty, lack of education and gender inequality—are also abundant, but that is not all. Under apartheid, such factors were severely exacerbated, and the forced break up of families and communities, and the high mobility of workers, encouraged a situation where many men engaged in unsafe sex with multiple partners while away from their families.

Eleven years after apartheid was formally dismantled, the scars are still visible in Khayelitsha, but new problems have surfaced where one might least expect them—from within the post-apartheid government of the African National Congress (ANC), which led the struggle for nonracial democracy in the country.

South Africa's new Constitution pledges the government to address the risk factors for HIV/AIDS, but performance is lagging behind principle. The Bill of Rights promises all citizens equal access to healthcare, food, water and social security. It also calls for equal rights to housing, a safe environment, access to information and the right to life. When it comes to HIV/AIDS, these rights ring hollow, as the government has responded slowly and often contrarily to the growing epidemic. This, in turn, has sparked a growing public outcry, led by organizations like the Treatment Action Campaign (TAC), which was founded in 1998 to carry out grass-roots education campaigns on HIV/AIDS and to pressure the government to respond to it more effectively.

The TAC has gone head to head with the ANC government through protests, debates and legal action. Its goal, say TAC activists, is to get affordable treatment and support for people living with HIV/AIDS and to develop education about HIV/AIDS prevention.

Before 2003, generic versions of ARVs were not available in South Africa, which meant that the vast majority of the population could not afford the drugs. After a 2003 TAC victory in court, generic ARVs became available, giving many people their lives back.

Noncedo, a TAC volunteer, says she tested HIV positive in 2001. Her doctor told her mother that she was going to die because treatment was not available. Today, she takes ARVs and lives a normal active life.

Many TAC volunteers are HIV-positive themselves, and they are passionate about education, prevention, and affordable treatment. They say they are holding their government accountable to the Bill of Rights, and they demand changes in the way the HIV/AIDS epidemic is being handled.

President Thabo Mbeki has long had a controversial stance on the issue. He has made statements doubting both that HIV and AIDS are connected and that HIV is sexually transmitted, despite overwhelming scientific evidence to the contrary. His health minister, Manto Tshabalala-Msimang, has also made questionable assertions about the value of good nutrition to treat HIV, instead of ARVs.

As a result, many South Africans do not know what to think. And they are scared.

Criticism against the government is a sensitive topic here. The ANC dominates the government with more than sixty-five percent of the seats in Parliament, and is held in high esteem for ending apartheid by most poor South Africans. "This is the movement that liberated them," says TAC field worker Mandla Majola. "If they stand up against the ANC, they betray."

And yet the ANC led government is falling short of its responsibilities, according to Majola, who says it is time now to ask the liberation movement new questions: "Yes, we can blame apartheid, but what are you doing as the present government?"

Majola says the government first needs to address the inequality that fuels the epidemic. He compares the differences in treatment for a black person living in Khayelitsha to that for a white person in Camps Bay, a wealthy Cape Town suburb. "These are two different worlds," he says.

The current de facto segregation is a vestige of the de jure segregation under the apartheid system. Majola says that a black person with HIV in Khayelitsha must live in a cold, leaky shack, go outside to get water, and use unsanitary community bathrooms, while a white person in Camps Bay lives in a warm, dry house with abundant fresh food and water, sanitary waste disposal, and much more. In Khayelitsha, one water tap serves 500 shacks, whereas in Camps Bay a single house may have up to thirteen.

"These are realities that affect us. They affect our health, our well-being," says Majola.

But the HIV/AIDS epidemic in South Africa is not just fueled by poverty and inequality—it is also propelled by neglect and denial.

"Many people have died because of denialism," says Majola.

The problem starts with widespread popular ignorance about the epidemic, according to the TAC activist. Public education about HIV/AIDS only came about in the late 1990s, after the problem had reached labor-force threatening proportions. At that point, many people still had not heard about AIDS, and those who had often held views at odds with the international scientific consensus. Mixed signals from the government only made things worse.

"I came across the word AIDS in 1998," says Majola.

In 1999, when his aunt died, Majola discovered a letter that revealed she had been HIV-positive. The next year Majola learned he, too, was HIV-positive. It was not easy to accept this, but he says he had to: "You can't run away from it. It's like the pigment of your skin. You accept it."

Majola says he dealt with his status by asking himself what he could do to help fight the epidemic, rather than getting frustrated and blaming others. Like many TAC volunteers, he dedicated himself to educating others. "In a way it was a blow, but I took it in a positive way. I have HIV," he says.

Majola, Zeldah, and Noncedo, among others receiving ARV treatment through MSF and TAC, say they find the messages from the government counter-productive and dangerous.

Adding to the confusion, the California-based Rath Foundation, headed by Dr. Matthias Rath, a German-born physician who promotes intensive vitamin therapy as an alternative to ARVs to treat HIV/AIDS, has begun to play a prominent role in ANC policy-making circles. In Khayelitsha clinics and TAC offices, the mere mention of Dr. Rath's name makes people's hair stand on end. One woman shakes her head in anger; another scoffs with a bitter laugh.

"That man is killing people," says Majola. "That man is confusing people, and it is causing unnecessary death."

Rath claims that ARVs, especially zidovudine (AZT), are toxic. He insists that the key to fighting HIV/AIDS is good nutrition using vitamins he produces and markets. He has also launched a smear campaign against the TAC, say TAC leaders.

President Mbeki and Tshabalala-Msimang have also publicly cast doubt on ARV treatment, and neither has denounced Rath's claims, despite a consensus in the medical community against his approach. The upshot is that many South Africans find themselves wondering whom to believe—their government and Dr. Rath, or the medical community and the TAC.

For her part, Zeldah says that she is alive today because of ARV treatment, and she is not alone in feeling optimistic, despite the odds against her.

"We have defeated apartheid," says Majola. "We will defeat AIDS. Rest assured."

# HIV Affects More Than Those Who Are Positive

## By Christine Franey
### Cape Town, South Africa

A healthy individual has a CD4 cell count—measuring one's immune system function—of more than 800 per cubic millimeter.

A person is eligible for government-supported HIV treatment in South Africa with less than 200.

Zeldah's was fifteen when she first discovered she was ill.

By then, her body was covered with lesions and abscesses. When she arrived at the hospital, she was five-feet, seven-inches tall and weighed only sixty-one pounds.

After hospitalizing her, the doctors informed Zeldah that she was HIV positive and that she was infected with both tuberculosis and pneumonia.

Though Zeldah's experience is common in South Africa, it is rare in the United States, where antiretroviral drugs help stave off the descent from HIV to AIDS for years, if not indefinitely. Many Americans have difficulty imagining what Zeldah – and thousands like her – face every day of their brief, pain-filled lives.

Such encounters during a three-week visit to South Africa forced me to confront difficult questions not only about the depth and extent of the tragedy before me, but also about my own identity and values. As a privileged, white, American female, I was both welcomed and rejected.

> *Most days people are lined up throughout the day because there are too few health workers to deal with the case-load. Would-be patients may wait for three hours just to be seen.*

Yet often, when I showed genuine interest, I found people ready to share the most intimate details of their difficult lives.

I met Zeldah at a joint HIV-TB clinic in Khayelitsha, a sprawling black township outside Cape Town, where she was receiving treatment for her HIV. Originally from Johannesburg, she was sent here by her mother to live with her sister. Isaac Magwana, a twenty-five-year-old working with a nongovernmental organization called the Treatment Action Campaign (TAC), introduced me to her.

TAC was created in 1998 by Zackie Achmat, an HIV-positive activist who dedicated himself to winning affordable treatment for South Africans with the virus at a time when the government was reticent to provide it. Many TAC members are HIV-positive, but anyone interested in the cause is welcome, according to another TAC volunteer, thirty-three-year-old Mandla Majola, though he is also HIV-positive.

The cost of treatment for HIV with antiretroviral drugs (ARVs) is R4,500 per month per person ($700)—beyond what most South Africans can begin to afford.

Forty-two percent of the black population here — a category that includes people of African, Asian and mixed ancestry in the lexicon of the anti-apartheid movement – has an income of R1,000 ($155) per month or less, according to Julian May in his report "Poverty and Inequality in South Africa." A majority of HIV-positive people falls into this bracket.

Khaylitsha offers a case in point. On my walk to the clinic, I saw a gray, cloud-filled sky. Walking through the building, I passed endless rows of brown-skinned patients. My blue eyes met a sea of staring brown eyes.

I settled into a waiting room with a thin cement walkway separating four rows of hard wooden benches, all filled with patients. As I sat quietly, Isaac, speaking in Xhosa—a South African language laced with distinctive clicks—asked if anyone would be willing to talk with me.

One gray-haired man agreed. He sat in the back corner, near the closed windows with rain misting the glass. While he waited for his continued treatment for TB—his second time being infected—he said his name was Boy Welcome.

I asked my questions in English. He understood me but responded in his native Xhosa to Isaac, who translated the answers.

Boy Welcome sat patiently and removed his neatly folded green card from a worn plastic bag, identifying his personal information and chronicling his treatment. An X lay in each box, corresponding to one day of treatment.

For his first infection, he had six months of pills administered Monday through Friday, he said. Each re-infection translates into eight months of injections.

"I cannot sit," said Boy Welcome of the painful treatment process.

As Isaac listened and Boy Welcome waited, a woman spoke to him in Xhosa.

"She wants you to ask her how she feels," said Isaac.

I asked her.

Once she started, her words poured out in a torrent. This was Zeldah.

At the time of her hospitalization, she already knew she was HIV-positive. She became pregnant and had a baby in 1996—at seventeen years old. It died soon afterward. She learned then that the baby was HIV-positive, and so was she.

Zeldah met her current boyfriend after she discovered she was HIV-positive, and she told him early in the relationship. He accepted her as she was, and they remain together today. Many of her friends are also HIV-positive.

Zeldah has been on ARVs for five years. Her CD4 count is up again, which indicates a healthy immune system. Her virus is low—virtually undetectable—and she is healthy, but she spends much of her time at the clinic

Most days people are lined up throughout the day because there are too few health workers to deal with the caseload. Would-be patients may wait for three hours just to be seen, said Zeldah.

The clinic has four doctors, according to the site administrator, who identified herself only as Nompumelelo. Working in pairs, they have two days on and two days off during the week, and they work every other weekend.

"I basically do everything," she said, describing a routine in which she comes to work in the morning and organizes the cards and sorts the folders in order of importance, setting the sequence in which the patients will be seen by the doctors. For follow-up appointments for HIV patients, she takes out the ARVs. As the day continues, she takes blood and administers medication. On an average day, the clinic sees 120 patients, of whom eighty are HIV-positive.

Despite her busy schedule, she managed ten minutes to talk about her day. She apologized that no doctor was available. Nor was that sort of generosity unusual.

I was greeted with smiles and cooperation everywhere I went. Driving to the clinics, I saw people waving to me while they were walking on the street. Once there, most people were eager to share their traumas just as openly as Zeldah and Boy Welcome.

This came as a surprise.

Before traveling to South Africa, I told one American woman with whom I work about my plans, and she broke into a dance and asked if I would see Africans perform a rain dance. Her image of the continent was one of spiritual, primitive people living in tribes.

Another American man, older and educated, told me to be careful of the lions because they could eat me, though he was aware that I was going to stay in cities.

The ignorance of Americans and the stereotypes they held haunted me as I traveled across in a country where people seemed so determined to uphold their national motto: 'diverse people unite.'

It was not so much that I fit in, as that it did not seem to matter that I didn't. The experience of walking down a corridor or along a street with people staring at me heightened my self-consciousness. But my difference engendered more curiosity than hostility.

South Africans labeled, rejected, and at times welcomed me for the innate characteristics that make me, well, me—just as they are struggling to do with one another. And they are rightly proud of their ability to do so.

# Poor AIDS Patients Receive Life-Saving-Medicine

By Kate Lolley

Khayelitsha, South Africa

As Zeldah waits, she can hear the sound of rain hitting the tin sheeting of the roof. The room is crammed with people on small wooden benches.

Looking around, she encounters only blank stares, sporadic coughing and the quiet shuffling of feet. Despite it being a winter's day, the room is uncomfortably warm from the number of bodies pressed together in the cramped twenty-by-twenty-five-foot space.

Zeldah, twenty-six, has been waiting more than three hours to see the doctor in the Ubuntu clinic in Khayelitsha, a black township twenty miles outside Cape Town. Like most of the waiting patients, she is here to receive her daily dose of anti-retroviral medication (ARVs) to treat her AIDS.

The drugs must be taken every day to reduce the amount of AIDS virus present in the blood. When the viral load is decreased, the immune system can produce normal levels of T cells. A functional immune system can fight the opportunistic infections that would otherwise kill an untreated AIDS patient.

ARVs are not a cure for AIDS, but a way to control and live with the disease. Anti-retroviral combination therapy is used in patients in the advanced stages of AIDS.

ARVs are administered as "drug cocktails" in which two or three medications are

> "Zeldah lays the flier on the bench. With her brown eyes sparkling, she turns and says: "I am fine now""

taken at once. If only one is taken, the virus could mutate and become resist-ant to treatment. Taking more than one medicine at a time prevents this.

Ubuntu is a joint AIDS and tuberculosis clinic, since tuberculosis is a common infection in patients with AIDS. Most of patients who come to it have already been diagnosed, and are here for their prescriptions.

The walls of the clinic are covered with rainbow-colored posters of patients and testimonials to their success with anti-retroviral medications. Not so long ago, having access to these life-preserving drugs was impossi-ble to most patients in this township because of the high drug costs.

Zeldah, who asks her last name be withheld, is one of the lucky ones.

Zeldah initially decided to get tested for HIV after losing her hair, developing lesions on her hands, and forming thrush in her mouth. She was diagnosed with HIV in 1996 when she was pregnant. When her daugh-ter was born, doctors said she was also HIV-positive.

Zeldah was living in Johannesburg at the time she contracted the virus. There was no AIDS treatment available to those who couldn't afford the full-priced, name brand ARVs. Zeldah contracted meningitis and tuberculosis, and her daughter died — all because of the lack of treatment, she says.

Zeldah eventually heard about a pilot program outside of Cape Town that was giving ARV medication to AIDS patients who wouldn't normally be able to afford it. That is what brought her here.

Drug prices are the biggest stumbling blocks for the poor seeking access to AIDS treatment, say AIDS activists. Ubuntu is one of three Khayelitsha clinics in a pilot program run by Doctors Without Borders and the Treatment Action Campaign (TAC) to give poor AIDS patients access to ARVs.

Doctors Without Borders—also known as Médecins Sans Frontières (MSF)—is an international nongovernmental relief organization that sends doctors to areas in acute healthcare shortage. The Treatment Action Campaign, a local grassroots organization, works to provide AIDS patients with access to ARVs.

Before the pilot program was in place, little could be done for patients not able to afford ARVs, says Nompu Melelo, a former community health practitioner and now the assistant in charge at the Ubuntu Clinic.

"It was pathetic to work with AIDS patients before," says Ms. Melelo. "There was nothing that could be done for them."

"Before treatment was available, doctors would diagnose you, tell you how to live, and send you home," says TAC national secretary Mandla Majola. "You would go home and wait for your death day."

The Khayelitsha program is the first of its kind in South Africa. Skeptics had argued that the lack of infrastructure and resources might result in patients failing to take their medication. This could cause a development of virus strains resistant to the drugs. However, a new protocol simplified the drug therapy, used fewer lab tests and assigned patient-monitoring to nurses or outreach workers instead of doctors.

The collaborative efforts of MSF and TAC in this project were recognized in 2003 by the World Health Organization as a model of "the best practice in the implementation of antiretroviral therapy."

Since the program is a pilot, only residents of Khayelitsha are eligible. To qualify for treatment, Zeldah—already in the advanced stages of AIDS—left Johannesburg to live in Cape Town. Her weight had dropped to twenty-eight kilograms (sixty-one pounds), and her CD4 count, the standard measurement of the immune system, had plummeted to fifteen from a normal count of more than 800, she says.

The high cost of brand name drugs make ARV treatment extremely expensive. Though patents from leading drug companies block the production of cheaper alternatives, a few countries, including India and Brazil, have successfully bypassed patent laws to make generic ARV drugs for the poor in their countries. South Africa, however, has not taken this route, and, until recently, residents had to pay full price for ARVs, whether they could afford to or not.

That changed in 2001 when MSF and TAC collaborated with the Brazilian government to buy its generic ARVs, says MSF. This has dropped the price of treatment here per person/per day to less than half what it was, from $3.20 to $1.55, allowing twice the number to be treated.

The program began with approximately fifty patients. TAC estimates that the three clinics have now treated 2,000 adults and children with ARVs. The organization also reports that after three years on antiretrovirals, four out of five patients are still alive.

The clinic cannot meet the demand for its services from the approximately 50,000 residents with AIDS in Khayelitsha, according to Ms. Melelo, who says they see an average of 140 patients a day with a staff comprised of only three doctors and three professional nurses.

Days at the clinic begin at 5 a.m. when patients begin lining up to see the nurses, who arrive at 8 a.m. The staff pitches in where needed to keep the patient flow moving, says Ms. Melelo, who adds that she does everything from running the clinic to triaging incoming patient folders to organizing storerooms.

Zeldah, who has been here since 7 a.m., is still waiting to hear her name called at 10 a.m. A nurse enters and calls a name. Zeldah stops talking—hoping she will hear her own.

She does not.

Despite the interminable waits, the clinic is a place of hope in the sea of dilapidated shacks that comprise Khayelitsha. Its nearly 500,000 residents live in huts constructed from salvaged tin sheeting, plastic tarps, flattened oil cans, tar paper, used plywood, worn doors and old door frames.

The plywood and tin roofs are held in place by rocks that anchor them in severe weather. During rainstorms, residents toss pails of water onto the streets as if bailing a sinking boat.

Buckets are used in lieu of toilets and hand-carried to disposal sites. Water for washing, cooking and drinking is fetched from one of the town's waterspouts; each spout accommodates approximately 500 shacks. The roads surrounding the township are scorched with burn marks where residents have burned tires to protest these living conditions.

The name Khayelitsha means "Our New Home" in the Xhosa language. It was established by the apartheid regime in 1983 as a place to dump blacks after running them out of their townships close to the center of Cape Town. The township was laid out in a grid pattern to make it easier for police forces to patrol the area.

Struggles with the government continue today, eleven years after apartheid ended. While the provincial government supports the clinic by providing two of its doctors and covering a portion of the clinic's costs, the national government is a different story.

President Thabo Mbeki, who succeeded Nelson Mandela in 1999, has resisted the use of ARVs to combat AIDS, claiming they are too expensive for South Africa, and questioning the link between HIV and AIDS. This has put him at odds with international authorities like the World Health Organization, and has generated major protests within the country. It places him in peculiar company as he seeks to rationalize this approach.

Mbeki recently enlisted the help of scientist and fellow AIDS skeptic Roberto Giraldo to support his position, says Samantha Power, a lecturer in Public Policy at Harvard University. The South African Ministry of Health invited Giraldo to South Africa in January 2003. During his talk he mentioned the benefits that good nutrition can have on the immune system. Afterward, the Health Ministry announced that AIDS patients should consume "garlic, lemon, olive oil, and African potatoes" to help their immune systems.

"These things are affordable for South Africans," says the Ministry of Health, "not like things like antiretrovirals."

Today, many South Africans are confused about the disease due to the contradictory messages put out by the national government, say TAC volunteers. Some are baffled about its causes; others are in the dark about what sorts of treatment they should undergo.

One of TAC's main purposes is to educate and inform the public about the truth about AIDS and ARV treatment, according to its literature. TAC has nearly 15,000 volunteers in 300 branches in six of the country's nine provinces.

These activists work to educate people at the grassroots level about how to prevent transmission, how HIV is contracted, what the virus is doing to the body, what stages the disease goes through, what it means to live with disease, how to identify symptoms of secondary infections caused by HIV/AIDS, such as tuberculosis, cryptococcal meningitis or pneumonia, and what are appropriate medications.

"We give them an education to fight for their treatment," says Mr. Majola.

TAC says its volunteers also lobby for affordable ARVs in South Africa to stem the deaths of nearly 500 people each day due to the lack of access to affordable ARV medicine. Volunteers are protesting major pharmaceutical companies to convince them to either lower their drug prices or lift their drug patents in South Africa.

"If in this clinic there are no ARVs, it's my job to protest," says Mr. Majola. "That's violating my human rights, and I'm prepared to go to Parliament to defend my rights."

In 2003, the national government responded to this pressure with an announcement that ARV treatment would be available in every health district within one year, and in every local municipality within five years. TAC volunteers say they are working to ensure that this promise is carried out.

For her part, Zeldah is content to wait for her turn in one of the few programs that is up and running. "I'm here at the clinic everyday," she says with a smile. "My viral load is low now."

Suddenly, the waiting room door opens, and the sound of raindrops echoes through the entryway. A tall, clean-shaven man walks in wearing a dark suit and holding a stack of fliers. When Zeldah turns over the paper he hands her, she sees a banner headline: "Funeral Policy—only 35 rand."

Zeldah lays the flier on the bench. With her brown eyes sparkling, she turns and says: "I am fine now."

# TESTING TOLERANCE:
## AIDS ACTIVIST CLOSETED DESPITE "ACCEPTING" COLLEAGUES

BY ERIN ROOK
CAPE TOWN, SOUTH AFRICA

She steals a glance over her shoulder and confides in a hushed tone, "I had a girlfriend." She pauses for emphasis. "A girlfriend."

Her boyfriend is across the hall in another part of the office, so she must be discreet. He doesn't know about the girlfriend, or that Billy, whose name has been changed, is still attracted to women. No one does.

Though South Africa's Constitution prohibits discrimination on the basis of sexual orientation, many South Africans are not as accepting of difference. A recent survey by the Human Sciences Research Council of South Africa found that eighty-one percent of black South Africans feel that same-sex relationships are "always wrong."

In the predominately Xhosa township where twenty-three-year-old Billy lives, there is a similar dissonance between law and popular opinion. Misconceptions about gays and lesbians run rife, and many people are more concerned about day-to-day survival than fighting for gay rights.

Even though Billy works for South Africa's Treatment Action Campaign (TAC), a progressive HIV/AIDS activist group led by an openly gay man, Billy says she has never considered coming out to her friends and colleagues.

"There are girls [at TAC] who are open about their sexuality and they're okay with it,"

> *She never sought out a girlfriend—the relationship just happened. And even if she had wanted to find a woman to date, she would not know where to look.*

she says, "but they're not friends, they're colleagues." While TAC members profess tolerance and acceptance, Billy says it is easy for people to say they accept gays and lesbians when they are not friends with any.

But Billy is more than a colleague. In addition to dating a fellow TAC staff member, she is a close friend with Sabelo, another TAC activist whose name has been changd to protect Billy's identity. Though unaware of Billy's sexuality, Sabelo admits that there are still cultural barriers to accepting homosexuality.

"Homosexuality is still a taboo," he says. Some South Africans believe that homosexuality is a Western import, that "it is un-African. It is not religious. It is not godly."

But while Sabelo credits TAC for teaching him to accept differences, Billy says she is not sure how Sabelo and her other colleagues would react to her coming out.

"It's easy for you to say something when it's not close to you," she says.

Billy is especially concerned about how her boyfriend would feel if he knew that, despite being his girlfriend and the mother of a two-year-old girl, she often thinks of women when they are together.

## CURIOSITY

While she has had only one relationship with a woman, Billy says she often wonders what it would be like to be with another.

"I wish I could have another relationship and see where it takes me," she says. She never sought out a girlfriend—the relationship just happened. And even if she had wanted to find a woman to date, she would not know where to look.

"We actually met in the street," she says of her former girlfriend. "We sort of like clicked. I didn't know I had it in me." At first, she doubted her attraction, writing it off as simple admiration.

"I thought maybe I liked her as a friend," she says. However, "when she started having other friends, I started to get jealous, and she noticed. I also started getting approached by other girls."

What started with a kiss became a long-term relationship that lasted until the girlfriend moved away. Billy then started dating men again, though she says she is still interested in women.

"I sometimes have feelings for other girls," she says. "Sometimes I see someone and say 'Wow.' But I can't tell my boyfriend." He does know she had sex with a woman that once, but that is all—it was after this disclosure that she started imagining he was a girl when they slept together.

No one knows the whole story. She says she has not confided in a best friend because she does not have one—she believes that best friends "complicate things."

"I've never actually told anyone, not even a woman," she says. "Sometimes I'll admire a woman and my friends say, 'Be careful.'"

Her friends may be cautionary for a reason. While Billy has never told anyone the full story before, she does not work to hide it, and even drops clues here and there. However, Billy does not fit a stereotypical lesbian image, so she has never been seriously questioned.

"People suspected we were seeing each other, but they were not sure," she says. "Sometimes I go as far as to say I once did it. Everyone says, 'No, no' they don't believe me because I don't act like a man."

## STEREOTYPES

The fact that Billy has a child and sleeps with men further confuses those who might suspect her of being attracted to women.

"People think because you have a baby you can't be a lesbian," she says. She knows one lesbian who came out after the birth of her second child. But when people talk about her they make a point to say, "She's a lesbian—but she has two children."

As a woman who is attracted to women, Billy is full of paradoxes. While she does not explicitly define herself as a lesbian, she recognizes that society tells her she can either be a manly un-African childless lesbian, or a feminine black South African heterosexual mother.

But Billy falls somewhere in the middle.

"Sometimes I ask myself, am I this or am I that or am I both?" she says. "I don't know if I'm bisexual or what."

No one seems to notice this inner conflict, however, because Billy does not "look like a lesbian." She says that most out lesbians in Khayelitsha "act like men;" they wear big pants, drink, and smoke marijuana.

Many people, both gay and straight, seem to think that if a woman likes women, she should act like a man. But Billy says that some lesbians may act like men because they want to be identified as lesbians. However, "many women shave their hair and dress like men and see men. There's no way to know if someone is a lesbian."

In fact, Billy has known few lesbians personally. In addition to her former girlfriend, she knows two—a former friend and a woman she was once interested in. The latter is the only lesbian she knows of who does not act "manly." But because this woman did not fit the stereotype, Billy had to rely on subtle hints to know she was interested.

"This girl didn't look like a lesbian; she was into me," she says. "She kept giving me these hugs, squeezing me. I thought, I love her. But then she went for someone else."

Because homosexuality is still not acceptable in most South African townships, dating takes a bit of detective work. "What I've learned is that if I'm interested in someone, I fish for information," she says. For now, however, she will stay with her boyfriend, whom she describes as skinny, sensitive, and soft. But if she met a woman who caught her eye, she says she would never date them both at once.

"If I met a woman, I wouldn't tell my boyfriend about that woman," she says. "I would make the decision first and then leave him." It is unlikely she would ever leave him for another man, though, since she says she has little interest in having sex with men, including her own boyfriend.

### OUT IN THE WORLD

Billy figures that as long as she is in a heterosexual relationship, there is no need to disclose her attraction to women. If she were serious about a woman, she says she might tell someone. Until then, she doesn't want to confuse people.

"If I said I had feelings about a woman and then introduced them to a boyfriend, they would be confused," she says. Besides, it is a topic no one seems too interested in discussing.

Other than family discussions about whether same-sex marriage is immoral—its legalization is likely soon—Billy says homosexuality is something people just do not talk about.

Even in the office, where staff preach acceptance, she says it is "one topic they never talk about. They say, 'That lesbian so-and-so.' I might give Sabelo the benefit of the doubt, but what about the others?"

"They think they know me," she says. "We are pretty good friends, especially Sabelo. I think I can tell him anything but [the truth about her sexuality]." Though she has more faith in Sabelo than in the others, she is still uneasy because he is also friends with her boyfriend.

As for her female colleagues, she says that if they knew, they would not want to hug her anymore and would become suspicious of her motives. On the other hand, she says, they might even be offended if she tried to reassure them by saying she wasn't interested in them.

She said that if she were to come out now, instead of in her adolescence, people would see it as a trend or a new thing. Younger people, Billy thinks, are more easily accepted as gays and lesbians.

Still, there is a long way to go. Sabelo says that one of his own friends, an educated computer scientist, makes jokes about so-called "conversion rape" – the idea that a lesbian can be made straight through forced heterosexual sex, often gang rape.

One day, Sabelo was standing with this friend when a lesbian walked by and the friend said, "We need to organize five men to have sex with her, she'll be fine."

Billy says such sentiments are not uncommon. She has heard stories about a lesbian being raped and beaten, though she did not know about it personally. However, she adds, the victim acted like a guy and had a cocky attitude, as if to explain why she was attacked.

Perhaps this is why Billy says she would not be afraid of violence if she decided to come out as a lesbian.

"Maybe I'm too confident," she says. "These things also happen in other kinds of sexual relationships, but people don't notice it."

LGBTI (lesbian, gay, bisexual, transgender, and intersex) groups like the Triangle Project and Siyazenzela, both based near Cape Town, offer support for gays and lesbians living in townships. However, Billy says she has never heard of their outreach programs.

Billy says that people in Khayelitsha would not shy away from attending a same-sex marriage if one took place, but not out of support: "They would all go to see what a disaster it would be out of curiosity."

If that day does come, however, it will not be Billy at the altar. While she supports legalizing same-sex marriage, she says she is not interested in participating.

"Isn't marriage about love? It goes back to you, what you want and what you feel," she says. "I would never marry a man, and I would never marry a woman."

She says she simply is not interested in marriage, even if the right girl comes along—a possibility she is open to. But she is not going hunting.

"I don't want to go out there looking for a woman," she says. "When it happens it will happen and I will know it."

# Facing an
# Uncertain Future

# SOUTH AFRICAN YOUTH:
## FROM ACTIVISIM TO APATHY

BY EVAN KUHLMAN
JOHANNESBURG, SOUTH AFRICA

Noticeably absent from the university campuses here are the banners and picket signs that marked South Africa's fierce anti-apartheid struggle in the 1980s and early 1990s. Eleven years after the transition to democracy, the activism that drove the movement for equality has been overtaken by youth apathy.

"I'm very interested to see what kind of leaders come from my generation," says twenty-three-year-old Talia Sanhewe, a rising star in South African broadcasting who studied politics and media intensely, but who admits she is a rarity in her generation. Though she is interested in South African policy, many of her friends and peers could care less, she says.

"The attitude is very 'I don't know, I am a post-apartheid South African woman, I don't need to know,'" she says, mimicking the response from her friends.

"When it comes to careers they are very driven, but no one has any social consciousness," she says. "There isn't a lot of, 'How can I help on the greater scale?'"

Students are much less political than students were in the past, says former anti-apartheid newspaper editor and current University of Witwatersrand journalism professor Anton Harber, echoing Sanhewe. Now, students are focused on jobs, careers, passing school and just getting through.

> *While studying at school, she said she attempted to rally peers around an outbreak of rapes on campus without success: "We would have marches and demonstrations. But no one would come, they would just watch."*

"South African youth are very apathetic," Sanhewe says.

While studying at school, she attempted to rally peers around an outbreak of rapes on campus without success. "We would have marches and demonstrations. But no one would come, they would just watch."

Sanhewe's experience is not uncommon. While South African school children make field trips to the Hector Peterson Memorial where students protesting apartheid were massacred in Johannesburg, there are no new stories tellingof children and young adults standing up to injustices now.

"If they have clothes, a car, water, food, money—what more do they need," says another young South African woman who shares Sanhewe's concerns. Now in her late twenties, Duduzile "Dudu" Sibanyoni, who describes herself as an "activist," says she even notices a difference in the way she and her twenty-year-old brother talk about social issues.

However some students disagree.

"There is always something boiling underneath," says University of Cape Town (UCT) music student Akhona Ndzuta. According to Ndzuta, there is a growing concern about racism and violence against women, though she concedes that not all students seem to care.

The stereotype of South Africans being happy and gentle has hindered the understanding of future generations, she says.

"A lot of young people are ignorant, not purposely," Ndzuta says. The lack of communication from older generations has left a gap in the sharing of stories with South African young people.

UCT professor Paul Sedres agrees. "We are not big enough to teach young people about where we have come from," he says. "If you take a fifteen- year-old to Robben Island today, they cannot understand."

"It does not mean that we should carry other generations' pain and guilt. Maybe it's a good thing that the youth of today doesn't show much interest in the past," says Yolanda Tobin. "If generations ahead of you are people who aren't going to deal with it, how can a young person be expected to?"

# PERFORMANCE ISSUES: CRACKS SHOW IN THE RAINBOW NATION

## BY FAY STAMBUK
### JOHANNESBURG, SOUTH AFRICA

"After the elections I left the country for four years. I studied in England. I didn't mean to come back," says Mark Strijdom, twenty-six, a white Afrikaner who works at a music store in the Rosebank Mall.

As he explains his self-imposed exile, his fingertips flip CD after CD in search of urban South African music, known as Kwaito, the South African equivalent of Hip Hop.

The shop, a tiny cubicle, bursts with CDs. Its dark, sophisticated woodwork appears to suit Strijdom's diffident yet confident demeanor.

"I don't think it is good to erase history," he says, referring to a recent government initiative to alter names of streets and institutions put in place by the previous apartheid-era regime, opening a conversation that reveals a lingering dissatisfaction with the new government.

Meanwhile, some black South Africans think the new government is moving too slowly to right the wrongs of the past—or to deal effectively with new problems such as the rapidly escalating HIV/AIDS crisis—and some former anti-apartheid activists worry that the former liberation fighters now in power lack respect for democratic values.

All insist they support the present government, but their readiness to voice their concerns suggests that the honeymoon may be

> *People believe and trust the government, which gives them absolute power. And absolute power brings corruption.*

ending for the African National Congress (ANC), which dominates the political scene today and appears to have no serious challengers in the run-up to the next round of elections in 2009.

Formed in 1912 to promote the rights of the African people largely through nonviolent protest, the ANC took up arms in 1960 after it was banned and forced underground. Its continuing resistance, supported by extensive popular protests and punishing international sanctions, forced the white-run National Party (NP) to cede power to the disenfranchised black majority in the early 1990s. Since then, the ANC has held an overwhelming majority of seats in the parliament and has moved decisively to democratize the country. Among its successes is one of the most progressive constitutions in the world.

A political science student at the University of Johannesburg, Strijdom is the grandnephew of J.G. Strijdom, who headed the NP in the early years of apartheid and was the country's prime minister in 1954. His policies included the removal of "coloreds"—a South African term for people of mixed race—from the common voter rolls. He also served during the first round of "treason trials" that targeted 156 anti-apartheid activists, including Nelson Mandela.

"But don't get me wrong, I don't agree with any of his notions," says Strijdom of his notorious ancestor.

Ten minutes later he holds four CDs in his hands, opens one and puts it into the stereo. Fast, strong beats and spoken words bring alive the little room, as customers scamper in and out.

"But you know, affirmative action is another such topic," he says, as he searches for more South African CDs. "The aspiration was to collapse racial classifications, yet the ANC seems to go the other way."

"The affirmative action anarchy pushes out skilled and qualified labor while it instills a new mentality in the previously privileged, a sort of inferiority complex," he says.

Black businesswoman Thandi Marah, a long-time anti-apartheid activist with the ANC who now runs a black empowerment program for one of South Africa's largest corporations, Eskom, disagrees.

"I don't feel that affirmative action allows disqualified labor," she says. "But because education in many cases is still behind, firms are forced to employ those who at least have some future potential to fill the quota."

Meanwhile, the ANC faces criticism from its own supporters for violating the new constitution when it moved to suppress publication of press reports of corruption within its ranks.

Anton Harber, a former anti-apartheid journalist who teaches media studies at the prestigious Witwatersrand University in Johannesburg, says the ANC is very strict with criticism. "The ANC says it is still too young, and the media has to be patient, to give them time, to 'take it easy,'" he says. "Yet this causes immense controversy."

The question the media is left with, he adds, is: "How critical can one be?"

Mandla Majola, an employee at the HIV/AIDS Treatment Action Campaign (TAC) in Khayelitsha, Cape Town, goes further in his criticism. "HIV/AIDS treatments differ completely depending if you are white or black," he says. "In that sense, apartheid is still in place. Here in the township we don't have proper access to medication, private clinics, or even basic needs like running water and warm shacks; in parts of Khayelitsha up to 500 shacks share one water tap."

Such conditions violate the constitution, which says delivery of basic needs is a right, he says.

"The government lives in upper-class areas while it forgets about its own people," Mandla says. "They don't want to accept the realities. We waited for too long, but people are still attached to the ANC, the movement that liberated them."

"You know, these leaders have been in power for too long," says Strijdom. "They pat each other on the back, forget easily about the past, and unlearn how to think outside of the box."

"Besides, people believe and trust the government, which gives them absolute power," he says. "And absolute power brings corruption."

He smiles appreciatively to himself and adds: "Don't get me wrong. I know I may sound bitter, but I am not. I have great hope and see a lot of potential for this country. In the end, that's why I returned."

# Children in One Family Look Abroad for Jobs

By Lyly tran
Cape Town, South Africa

Anita Atherson addresses her eighteen-year-old son in Afrikaans, but he responds in English.

She says she does not try too hard to make her son speak her native language because he will leave her soon to find a job. And Afrikaans, she acknowledges, is not useful outside South Africa.

Anita tells a visitor this story as she serves a colorful platter of warm milk, sugar and steaming rooibos tea at the African Art Factory Café in the Victoria and Alfred Waterfront, a popular tourist gathering-place. She is not shy about sitting down for a leisurely talk, as there are no other customers at this moment with thick clouds promising afternoon rain.

Anita has been working here for a month. She says she got the job when a childhood friend introduced her to the management. She is grateful for the favor, though her workplace is not as glamorous as many cafés in this upscale mall. The furniture consists of picnic tables with chipped paint, and business is slow. The platter she serves costs only R3 (less than 50¢).

As soon as she sits, she asks for an e-mail address and a phone number to give to her son, Lyle, which she secures in her apron pocket. Afterward, she describes him as a tall, handsome boy, who is good with computers Her wide eyes glow with motherly pride.

> Her brother Lyle, who slouches comfortably on the sofa, wears a red T-shirt with a small Nike logo. His hair is in a crew cut. He says he is taking night classes in criminology but is unsure what type of job he wants-though he does not expect it to be in South Africa.

Lyle has a girlfriend from Taiwan, whom he talks with over the Internet, she says. He wants to leave the country when he has the money.

She does not want her son to leave her, but she says she wants the best for him. Her dilemma typifies that of many South African "coloreds"—people of mixed-race ancestry-who now see themselves caught in the middle of a transition from white power to black power in which they are fast losing ground.

Estimates of the unemployment rate in South Africa run as high as forty percent. Affirmative action programs provide opportunities for blacks with higher education, but for families classified as "colored," such as Anita's, this makes finding work extremely difficult.

Coloreds make up 8.9 percent of South Africa's population, according to the 2001 South Africa census. The Labor Force Survey reports that 21.8 percent of coloreds are unemployed, but its definition for this is narrow. The same survey indicates that black South Africans face an unemployment rate of 31.3 percent and whites, 5.4 percent.

Later, at her house in Woodstock on the other side of Cape Town, Anita takes an American visitor on a tour of the home to which she moved recently, and introduces her nine-year-old daughter, Nikita, who has sat peering out the window for two hours awaiting their guest. The spacious living room is decorated with watercolor reprints and outfitted with a sophisticated stereo system, and the neighborhood is safer than where they came from.

Nikita talks eagerly about the fourth grade, but says she dreams of visiting Disney World some day. After meeting her brother's girlfriend, she says she loves Asian culture and wants to visit China, too. Anita adds that Nikita—who is slender and has her mother's large eyes and wavy, coffee-colored hair—always looks for things with Asian calligraphy.

Her brother Lyle, who slouches comfortably on the sofa, wears a red T-shirt with a small Nike logo. His hair is in a crew cut. He says he is taking night classes in criminology but is unsure what type of job he wants, though he does not expect it to be in South Africa. At present, he is enamored with New York City.

Seated next to Lyle, their cousin Ryan, sixteen, says he wants to join his relatives in New Zealand when he finally looks for a job.

The choice of these destinations is typical, according to South Africa's Migration Policy Institute, which says the most common countries to which South Africans emigrate today are the U.K., the U.S., Canada, Australia and New Zealand. An estimated 20,000 skilled workers and educated professionals left the country in the three years after apartheid ended in 1994, creating what some call a "brain drain." And the drain continues, the institute says.

Anita's husband Brian blames much of this on black empowerment programs—South African's version of affirmative action—especially for those like him who are classified as "colored." Though he says he was against apartheid, he says he was able to find jobs then, making three times as much as he does today.

He is employed now, but he is not happy with his job, and he worries that his options are closing. He works with the computer language Powerhouse, but says it is practically extinct. He is qualified to work in the Department of Education, but cannot find a job there.

"I've applied to two jobs which fit my qualifications to a T," Brian says, adding that he was not given either. Instead, they went to blacks who, according to him, were not qualified.

South Africa's new Employment Equity Act was designed to "redress the disadvantages in employment" of certain groups through affirmative action and the elimination of discrimination. Brian says that this law is to blame for his underemployment.

When whites were in charge, he says, they had the advantage for jobs. Now that blacks are in charge, he says, they have the advantage.

In fact, he goes on, coloreds are worse off now than before. In post-apartheid South Africa, with the old hierarchy flipped upside down, coloreds are still in the middle, but now there are more people on top pressing down.

"If the government gives preference to just one or two percent of blacks, they'll push all coloreds out of the job market," Brian says, placing his hand high in the air to represent blacks and indicating that his elbow represents whites, while coloreds are lost in the middle.

"It should be like this," he says, tilting his arm horizontally.

Like Anita, Brian does not savor his children's exodus. But if things continue as they are, he says, they stand no hope of finding a job in South Africa.

"I have a lot of hope in my son," he says, leaving out the front door.

# Successful Women
# Walk a Fine Line

## By Darline Tunis
## Johannesburg, South Africa

"If you're a black woman in South Africa, you've got your bread buttered on all four sides," says SABC-FM assistant producer Talia Sanhewe, now in her mid-twentyies and rising rapidly in her profession.

"I wish I were younger," says lawyer and business owner Nothemba Nlonzi. "There are plenty of opportunities for women."

Disparities still exist, says technology specialist Mpumi Majavu. But the trend is changing with government-supported affirmative action policies that give priority in hiring first to black women, then to disabled women or men, black men, and white women before white men are considered.

"A female engineer will earn equal to or more than a male engineer now," she says. "Even single women are now earning the same or more than their married male counterparts. Companies go the extra mile to attract women of caliber and color."

Men may still hold most executive positions, but women are rapidly moving up the ranks, according to many aspiring black professionals—especially if they are young and single. However, for those with families, the main problems are no longer in the workplace but at home.

"Men would rather not work if women make that much money," says businesswoman Nhlannhla Mjoli-Mncube, adding that she lives

> "If you're a black woman in South Africa, you've got your bread buttered on all four sides."

near a golf course filled with unemployed husbands enjoying a game while their wives are at work.

The two women, former activists in the African National Congress, are panelists in a roundtable on black women in business at the Rosebank Hotel. With them are Thandi Marah, the former Women's National Coalition director who now runs a black empowerment program for South Africa's largest utility, Eskom; Nothemba Mlonzi, who heads Women in Oil and Energy, a nongovernmental organization set up with Thandi's help; and city planner Noviwe Qegu. All are veterans of the anti-apartheid struggle. They look the part they now play.

One wears a blue linen suit complemented by a striped collar shirt. Another has on black slacks and a chic red blazer outlined in white. A third wears a blue-and-gold suit made of African cloth. The fourth sports a traditional navy blue blazer over a khaki dress. The last is in the essential black pantsuit. They are trailblazers in the fields of information technology, construction and finance, business, politics and law.

Among them, they hold degrees from the University of Cape Town, the University of the Witwatersrand, the University of Transkei, and the Boston-based Massachusetts Institute of Technology. In addition, they take part in numerous community self-help organizations, and are wives and mothers. Which is where complications arise.

As powerful as they are in their respective positions, they must carefully balance their roles as career women and traditional African mothers and wives. Even when their husbands are supportive, friends and neighbors are often critical—usually of the husband.

"If you're a woman with power, your husband is a sissy. He lets you out of his control," says Mjoli-Mncube.

Mjoli-Mncube says that while living in the U.S. as an employee in the construction and finance sector, she made more money than her husband. In fact, she says, he was not working, and the relationship was "fantastic."

However, in South Africa, this can create difficulties. "If I make more money than my husband," says Majavu, "he may leave because he is not in control."

"There's always a compromise," says panel moderator Thandi Marah.

As a wife and mother of three children, Marah is constantly busy. Her husband, a West African Muslim, is very supportive at home, but she says that in the presence of her in-laws he cannot prepare the day's meal. Nor can she appear in the clothing she normally wears to work.

Balancing is difficult, says Marah. Outside the home, she is a feminist, but inside her husband wants her to be his wife first. So she has to be outstanding at both vocations to succeed. She has early mornings and long days but must manage her time to meet the needs of workplace and family.

At one point, activist-turned-tour-guide-and-entrepreneur Shereen Habib did not manage her time so that her family would not suffer. She vividly remembers leaving her husband at home in Cape Town's Bo-Kap district when she launched her tourism business in the city's Malay Quarter. Soon after, she started receiving notes from her children asking, "Mommy, when are we going to see you?"

"I wasn't marketing my business only. I was marketing my country, my people, my community," says Habib, adding that she took her work seriously because she had a mammoth task on her hands, trying to use the new business to educate visitors about the social, cultural and political issues that had defined her life until then as an ANC supporter and, at one point, even an ANC candidate for Parliament.

With the death of her husband three years ago, all of that changed as she found herself the sole caretaker for her children. "My husband was one hundred percent behind them. When he was no longer there, I would be needed more," she says. "He covered for me so much, and I was now going to have to slow down."

Nor is the situation less complicated for women in the world of politics.

Ncumisa Kondlo's stylish black pantsuit and powder-blue-collar shirt are standard for a Member of Parliament. So is the pantsuit with a burnt orange collar shirt worn by Connie September, another MP. Both are prominent ANC leaders who spent much of the apartheid years underground or abroad. However, Kondlo says she cannot visit her in-laws dressed like this. Nor is she to appear in public without her head covered.

Though her profession requires professional dress, traditional African society demands conservative garb and a covered head. She says she was once chastised by an older man after she was seen on television working with her head unclothed.

Many men are also finding it difficult to adjust to the new gender roles, especially without the support mechanisms available to women.

"Males are marginalized by the women/female empowerment movement," says Grace Khunou, a doctoral student at the Wiser Institute of Witwatersrand University researching gender roles and identities.

"The plight of women is on the forefront," says Khunou. "But men still need help being men and dealing with the empowered woman."

"Challenging men to change affects their privilege, and therefore identity," says Kgamadi Kometsi, another doctoral student at the Wiser Institute studying gender roles. "A threat to manhood is a threat to personhood."

Programs such as EngenderHealth and Men as Partners, non-profit agencies educating men on reproductive health and gender equity, are aiding in the effort to change gender roles.

"I realized how much freer I could be when I didn't have to be doing what has supposedly been men's role," says one Planned Parenthood Association of South Africa health educator.

"This is still the beginning," says Marah. "There is a long way to go."

# BIRTHING A
# NEW CULTURE

# Retelling the Story of a Language
# Afrikaans in the New South Africa

By Jen Daniels
Cape Town, South Africa

Three granite obelisks rise into the air in Paarl, forty miles north of this bustling port city, to commemorate the 1865 recognition of Afrikaans as a distinct language and to honor the continents from which it originated: Europe, Africa, and Asia.

The hyperbolic Afrikaans Language Monument stands next to the Afrikaans Museum, which honors the Afrikaner nationalist movement and features material on the Association of True Afrikaners, which first wrote the language down.

The Slave Lodge, in the heart of Cape Town, tells another story—that of the slaves the Dutch brought here from Asia. Inside, the Iziko Human Rights Museum credits the slaves not only with physically building South Africa's early infrastructure, but also with contributing to the creation of the Afrikaans language.

During the apartheid era, Afrikaans was an important feature of Afrikaner identity as well as a potent symbol of oppression for the country's disenfranchised majority. However, in the post-apartheid national reconciliation process, efforts are underway to reclaim the language so it, too, can contribute to South Africa's new, multicultural identity. Certainly its roots run deep through the country's tortured history.

When the Dutch East India Company came to South Africa and formed the Cape

> *In the time of apartheid one could distinguish class position by the language people spoke-English was the language of affluence, while those in the working class spoke Afrikaans.*

Colony in the 1620s, it traded with the indigenous Koisan people and brought slaves from its other colonies in East Asia—places like Sri Lanka, Indonesia, and coastal India—and from African sources that were part of the Atlantic slave trade, like Madagascar and Mozambique.

Those from East Asia spoke Malayu. Assimilated from the great trading empires that had passed through the region, Malayu was an amalgamation of Arabic, Portuguese, and Dutch. It became the trading language of the East.

Arab traders brought their language to the East during the pinnacle of the Arab empires, between the eighth and the eleventh centuries. The Portuguese empire came next in the fifteenth and sixteenth centuries, reaching from East Asia to China to Africa. By the sixteenth and seventeenth centuries, the Dutch began to penetrate the region.

Both the Portuguese and the Dutch used Africa as part-trading post, part-penal colony for dissenters in their colonial holdings. Malayu became common among convicts and slaves all the way from East Asia to the eastern coast of Africa.

Indeed, today it is easy to recognize many Afrikaans words derived from Dutch, Portuguese, and various Eastern languages, says local history guide Mervyn Wessels. Words like baatjie (jacket), piesang (banana), and hemp (shirt) are similar to corresponding words in other languages.

Over time, the native Koisan people merged into European society. Many of their descendents were labeled as part of the "colored" class under the apartheid regime. Today, sixty-five percent of Capetonians can trace their ancestry to the Koisan, Wessels says.

After the British freed the slaves in 1838, their skills led them to become the artisans of Cape Colony. However, as more people with European ancestry arrived, the government legislated what jobs non-whites could hold. As a result, the descendents of the Koisan and the slaves formed the base of the colony's working class.

In the time of apartheid one could distinguish class position by the language people spoke. English was the language of affluence, while those in the working class spoke Afrikaans.

White Afrikaners trace their roots to the Dutch settlers of the Cape Colony and the French farmers that later settled there, though most commentators say that any notion of "racial purity" is a myth and that all Afrikaners are likely to be racial and ethnic montages.

In fact, Afrikaans itself is but the written form of a spoken language that emerged from the mouths of slaves, says Wessels. Indeed, the first known Afrikaans writing is in Arabic script.

Whatever their precise origins, Afrikaners have worked to preserve their heritage ever since the British came to dominate South Africa.

In 1919 Afrikaner nationalists founded the clandestine Broederbond (Brotherhood) to protect their rights and advance their position. It was when Broederbond supporters rose to power in 1948 with the election of the Afrikaner-controlled National Party that the system of racial separation known as apartheid was formalized.

Since apartheid's end in 1994, radio and television markets have been flooded with Afrikaans language, media targeting the white Afrikaner population, says Wessels. Driving down the highway, signs for early morning radio shows in Afrikaans stretch high overhead. Periodical stands carry newspapers in English and Afrikaans, and music stores have a separate rack for Afrikaans pop.

In the township of Soweto outside Johannesburg there is a large photo of a man, his face an expression of anguish. He carries a thirteen-year-old boy named Hector Petersen. His sister walks next to them, down the dirt road. She is also in anguish.

The photo was taken during the 1976 rioting in Soweto, when students walked out of schools to protest the imposition of the Afrikaans language as the language of instruction in public schools. Petersen was the first casualty when police opened fire on the protestors.

"We have a different attitude to the language than people in Soweto," says Wessels, a Cape Town native. He, too, can trace his family's ancestry to the Koisan people. In his own family, one of his daughters speaks English, while the other prefers Afrikaans.

# WESTERN FASHIONS THRIVE IN SOUTH AFRICA

BY GINA PATTERSON
CAPE TOWN, SOUTH AFRICA

Late on a cool Saturday night, black, white and Indian women and men mingle in line waiting to get into the popular hip hop club 169. Zulu and English fill the air as the line grows longer and longer.

The bass of the hip hop blares, and everyone shouts the words to 50 Cent and Beyonce.

Many of the men climbing the steep mahogany stairs wear fitted designer denims–GAP, Levis, Armani–and brightly colored Lacoste tees. They shout to one another in glee about the night's turnout.

Women tiptoe up the stairwell with high stilettos or Ugg boots. Hip-hugging jeans and tight shirts accentuate their curves. They walk by each other with cattiness in their eyes.

Western fashion has seeped into traditional South African culture to the point that people now have to make the decision to stay traditional or become "modern."

In the country's largest city, Johannesburg, many older men stroll through the popular, upscale Rosebank Mall in formal clothing— tight fitting dress pants and a collared white shirt. They accessorize with black loafers, black socks to match and fedora hats.

Older women wander through the mall with long navy blue skirts and collared white shirts, giving themselves a uniform look. Many have nude stockings, flat Mary Jane shoes, and oversize "Grandma" pocketbooks.

> She stands out in a sea of young girls with revealing clothes, which hint at the change in their morals. These too have been influenced by Western culture.

Men and women who were part of the apartheid generation have maintained their traditional identity, avoiding the latest Western fashion trend. Though they were Western-influenced in the past, they do not appear concerned with keeping up now.

Men and women of the post-apartheid generation are more focused on keeping up with the latest Western fashion trend. But this Westernized culture has infiltrated more than just style.

Ladies parade around Club 169 toting the best matching handbags from European designers like Louis Vuitton, Marc Jacobs, and Balenciaga. "Last year it was the Louis Vuitton; this year it is this bag," says one sales associate, pointing to a Balenciaga bag. Prices of genuine designer bags are normally thousands of dollars, but these are the equivalent of $100, signaling that they are not what they pretend to be. Nevertheless, knock-off bags appear to satisfy the craving of some young people for European fashion and culture.

By way of contrast, red and yellow hues splash over the long pleated skirt hiding all hint of legs and feet on one traditionally dressed passerby. A long-sleeved shirt hides the woman's arms, and a makeshift, color-coordinated crown covers her hair. She stands out in a sea of young girls with revealing clothes, which hint at the change in their morals. These too have been influenced by Western culture.

The percentage of people waiting to have sex until marriage is very small, according to community organizers for the Treatment Action Campaign (TAC), a national group that advocates treatment for people with HIV/AIDS. Khayelitsha, an impoverished city outside of Cape Town, has been one of the hardest hit cities with a high percentage of teenage sex, they say.

"If we are frustrated with watching TV, we are in our shacks making sex," says TAC representative Madla Majola. With limited resources, teenagers turn to the older generation with questions about sex but are often ignored. Traditional taboos on talking openly about these issues dictate the responses of the older generation, so young people now look to peers, pop culture, and the media for answers.

Women in low-cut bikinis gyrate back and forth on television screens. Smiling men emulate the actions of their favorite American rap stars. Traditional African beats have been replaced by imported rap and R&B stars. In clubs like the 169, men and women know more rap lyrics by California and New York-based performers than South African artists. On a Saturday night there are no traces of South African beats or jazz.

In much of urban South Africa, indigenous dialects have been overcome by English, which is taught as an instructional language in the national school curriculum. Students can only learn another language as an elective. During the apartheid era, the Afrikaans language was imposed on people in the schools and in official business. Now British and American English is pushing aside the African languages spoken by the country's majority, driven largely by the power of Western culture in the marketplace.

Outside the 169 Club, a car horn beeps, and a tall, young black man hops into a Mercedes sedan. It is another sign that what many young people want is to keep up with the latest Western trends. To be rich and own a condo and a BMW is their new dream, says Talia Sahewe, a highly successful young black woman professional.

"When it comes to careers, black people are ambitious, but when it comes to social consciousness—it's all about the bling-bling," Sanhewe says.

# FUNDA MEANS "TO LEARN"

## BY CHRISTINE FRANEY
## SOWETO, SOUTH AFRICA

Pauline Mazibuko apologizes for arriving late to speak with a visiting student group about her struggle as an artist in South Africa. She has just come from burying the father of her children.

"These are my bodyguards," says Mazibuko with an ironic smile, pointing to the two small boys beside her as she enters the canary-yellow gallery whose inside walls are covered with work from students at Funda, a fine-arts community college from which she graduated. Funda is set in the heart of South Africa's largest black township, Soweto. Its name means, "to learn" in Xhosa and Zulu.

It is to show her son how strong she is—and to honor a commitment to Funda administrators who supported her when she attended the school in the 1990s—that she is here today, she says.

Throughout her life, Mazibuko has struggled to support herself, but the unexpected death of her partner, coupled with the dire state of the South African economy—where the United Nations reports that black unemployment tops forty percent—raises the bar. Nor is this made easier by the fact that most of her friends and neighbors do not think that what she does—art—is a serious way to earn a living.

Mazibuko says she is always fighting to prove that making art is a legitimate—and potentially money-making—career for a black

> *She returns frequently to find her father angry at the children for extending their creativity from the paper to the walls themselves*

woman in a community that views females as having two main roles: child-bearers and homemakers.

She is here today to share her trials—and her unquenchable optimism—with a group of journalism students from Simmons College, an all-women's school in Boston. She says she is doing so at the request of Funda founder and director Charles Nkosi, whom she deeply respects for his efforts to support aspiring artists.

Mazibuko is one of his success stories—if measured by the recognition she receives, not the monetary rewards. Since leaving Funda, she has traveled with her art as far as Ethiopia, France, and Portugal. Yet she still lives in a shack.

Though the legal separation of blacks, 'coloureds,' Asians and whites known as apartheid ended in the mid-1990s with the election of a black-majority government and the ratification of a constitution guaranteeing equality for all, de facto segregation still flourishes, and most black South Africans continue to live in poverty.

Mazibuko currently resides in an extension of her parents' shack in an all-black community created by the apartheid-era government to enforce racial segregation. At that time, blacks were also relegated to second-class schools where they received what the government called "Bantu education," designed to train them for menial jobs in the white-dominated economy.

But Mazibuko was lucky—her school offered an art class. And she came from a family whose breadwinners had long practiced creative trades—her father as a builder and her grandfather as a carpenter. Nevertheless, despite her own creativity and that surrounding her, she says she did not think of art as a potential career until much later.

She originally trained to be a social worker because she wanted to help people, she says. But when she did decide that art was her true calling, she changed direction quickly. However, she came up against a wall of resistance from where she least expected it—at home.

When she informed her father that she would be attending Funda, he told her to move out of the house. But when she began to sell her artwork, he changed his attitude.

Next, she had to deal with her boyfriend. "If we get married and put the ring on your finger, then you must give up your art," he told her at the time of their engagement. He argued that she belonged to him because he paid "lobola" for her – a dowry given to the bride's parents, traditionally in the form of cattle but now in money.

Mazibuko sold a piece of her artwork, paid him back his money, and told him that now she was a free, single woman. They stayed together, but she never married him.

Meanwhile, her art took off. She now sells her collages for up to R15,000 ($2,500), using her own sacrifice and struggle as a source of creativity. She also paints, sculpts, and designs clothing.

"I try to portray what I feel," she says. "Everything just happens."

People tell her they see pain in her art, but she is quick to say that it is not all hers. She says that her art focuses on what she sees around her—like rape and the frequent abuse of women and children. One of her latest collages is constructed out of torn magazine pages that reveal two women's faces with pained expressions.

As for clothing, she says she only designs for herself and her sisters. Each piece is an individual work of art; she does not duplicate her creations. For one skirt, she used crepe and formed the shape of animals for protection.

When doing her art, Mazibuko says she jumps from one piece to the next, working on as many as five or six at once. She uses her bedroom for a studio and often draws her children into the process by covering the walls with paper and encouraging them to draw and paint beside her.

Sometimes they fight over her brushes, she says. But the real problems come when she is not at home.

She returns frequently to find her father angry with the children for extending their creativity from the paper to the walls themselves. Mazibuko says she does her best to wash off the color before it sets, but she is not always successful.

Of the two children, only one is her own—Sicalo ("wishing" in Xhosa), a name she says her deceased husband chose in anticipation of the arrival of their first child.

The girl, whom she treats as her second child, is the daughter of her deceased sister, she says. And, together, she adds, they are the reason she remains strong.

"If I go down, he goes down," says Mazibuko, looking at her son with a smile on her face and tears in her eyes.

# DRAWING ON PAIN TO HEAL

By Alexandria Carithers
Soweto, South Africa

Sibongile rolls up her sleeve and reveals her deepest secret—a dark red welt, long since healed but still broadcasting hurt.

She never lets anyone see this, says her sister Nelsie.

The scar is a constant reminder of their abusive childhood. It still hits them both hard today.

Sibongile fights back tears that seem seconds away from cascading down her cheeks as she tells her story. She shifts her eyes to the scar, then away. The pain is evident in her eyes as she blinks heavily.

The six-inch gash that once penetrated deep into her forearm and now resembles multiple gun shot wounds brings back vivid memories of the abuse both sisters suffered from their father and their half-brother throughout their childhood, she says.

"No, don't do that. She doesn't need to see that," says Nelsie, grabbing Sibongile's arm. Yet it is the depth and intensity of Nelsie's own pain that fuels her creative drive and provides much of the content for her unsettling works of art.

Nelsie Ndimande is a sculptor who recently graduated from the FUNDA Art Institute in Soweto, South Africa's largest black township, near where she grew up. She now makes a modest living selling her work, which she uses to address a range of women's issues, many of them deeply personal.

> They use their trauma as creative inspiration and the process itself as a way of healing.

Both Nelsie and Sibongile have two names, reflecting the conflicted heritage of many black South Africans. Nelsie, who goes by her Christian name, is also called Thulisiwe, meaning "someone who makes you quiet." Sibongile, who uses her African name, which means "thank you," is also known as Princess.

As Sibongile recounts her abusive past, she describes the wooden object she was struck with. Gesturing toward a nearby gift shop with her index finger, she points out a long, thick wooden cane in the corner and says only: *sjambok*.

The sjambok is a heavy whip-like weapon that was often used by police against anti-apartheid protestors in the 1980s. But, for Nelsie, the connection with the brutality of that era is more than ironic.

Many women artists who survived apartheid still face struggles in their personal lives, which they portray through their work. They use their trauma as creative inspiration and the process itself as a way of healing. Topics include HIV/AIDS, rape and domestic violence, cancer, and abortion.

When Nelsie's parents died—father from stroke and mother from natural causes—she took on the responsibility as mother to her four siblings, providing for her family by buying food and clothing, and trying to be a stable person whom her siblings could look up to as a role model.

Nelsie's mother, who worked as a maid, was a housewife and a strong black woman who did what she could for her children. As a domestic worker, she wanted to support Nelsie in the arts, but did not have the resources to do it, so she collected pieces of trash for her that she thought was art. "My mother tried to support me but did not know how," says Nelsie.

Her first encounters with art were drawings in children's books and biology textbooks, where she learned to draw maps and animals. Both she and her mother knew of her talent, but neither imagined art as a profession, Nelsie says.

However, Nelsie had a close friend involved at FUNDA, who introduced her to Charles Nkosi, the head of the art department there. This allowed Nelsie to get her foot into the arts scene.

Nelsie attended FUNDA for four years, majoring in sculpture. Through art she explored her long-hidden personal pain and gradually broadened her approach to tackle other women's issues, "I wanted to know what women experience in their daily lives," says Nelsie.

Nkosi was quick to recognize this drive in Nelsie and in other black women artists, and he supported their efforts. "These ladies have been a part of the fabric of the institution," he says now.

He also encourages the women to take these new skills into the marketplace, despite the difficulties they face there.

"We are the first to enter into this tough industry as women because it is known as an industry for men," says Nelsie. "We are so tough."

This toughness is immediately apparent in her art, which provides snapshots of her life. In one installation, an umbilical cord hangs loosely from a toilet, as handprints of blood cover the surface of the walls and the sink.

Women do not have access to resources that enable them to safely abort unwanted babies, so they resort to dangerous, "traditional" measures, says Nelsie. For example, women mix Dettol—a household disinfectant—with vodka, boil them together and drink the toxic brew to "get rid of the baby."

The art piece with the most personal meaning in Nelsie's life, though, is a rape scene. A woman lies powerless on the ground among the leaves and dirt. Torn clothing is scattered about. Her face is covered with a piece of cloth, as if to shield her from the trauma. Only half her torso is visible, with nails hammered in the vagina.

Nelsie says she drew inspiration for this from a tragedy that struck one of her friends.

While walking home from a local tavern one night, just miles from her home, the woman was kidnapped by a group of boys who dragged her into a ditch and repeatedly raped her. Afterward, Nelsie's friend found out that she had contracted HIV from which she later died.

The act of creating was therapeutic for Nelsie, she says. But she also wants to use her art to reach others.

"We as women are celebrating our independence. We know how to think for ourselves and do things for ourselves. Sculpting was something that was done by men, but now I can do it as a woman, and no one will be against it," says Nelsie.

# Speaking Out for Personal Freedom

## By Jen Daniels
### Cape Town, South Africa

On a Saturday night they come together in a bustling waterfront club to bare their souls—to publicly acknowledge their shared agony from problems whose existence has long been downplayed, if not denied outright, as the nation struggled to overcome the racial oppression that defined South Africa for decades.

Four young artists perform original material at the Ikhaya Soul Sessions, presented by a new promotional group, Urban Voices. They speak from personal experience about rape, child abuse, domestic violence, poverty, and homelessness, whose prevalence, only recently recognized, are taking on the dimensions of a major social crisis here.

"If you think about poetry and where it comes from—it's the basis," says one Urban Voices organizer who identifies herself only as Choki. "Poetry has been around as a means of entertainment and expression. I feel it's an outlet."

Today in South Africa, members of the activist anti-apartheid generation often accuse those too young to remember apartheid of being politically apathetic—partly because they don't recognize the new forms the post-apartheid generation chooses for its struggles. Many are addressing the social issues they confront today through a different kind of activist medium: the spoken word.

> "We are one. We are powerful as one diverse, one nation, one continent, one people, one, one, one AFRICA! But the battle has only begun."

"Everything stems from something," says Choki, twenty-three, who uses a nickname because she thinks her full name is just too hard for foreigners to pronounce. Choki and her friend Giselle started Urban Voices because they see a need for a forum through which young people can express themselves. They are not targeting a specific demographic, but young professionals are the main group to respond, she says.

"Story-telling leads to poetry, a story being written because people need to express themselves, and you can have music behind it, and you start speaking faster and then it's rapping," says Choki. While some performers at the Soul Sessions, held at the Ikhaya African Restaurant, have already achieved commercial success, others just come to express how they feel.

Some performers rap; others read poetry. They include a young man named Winslow, featuring guitarist Insense Instereo, Another, apparently unknown to the audience, identifies himself as Mbali. Two performers have already attained commercial recognition: Lu Chase, shortly to release her first album, and Burni, of the hip hop group Godessa.

Choki is from Mmabatho in northern South Africa, near the border with Botswana. She says her career has nothing to do with activism as conventionally defined. She came to Cape Town to attend the Peninsular Technikon Institute to study graphic design. She now works for an advertising company as a graphic designer.

Choki says she has always had an interest in performing spoken words, but never had the platform to do it. She adds that performing is not possible for her for the moment—without explaining why—but she says that organizing a forum for it was always something she wanted to do.

Her partner Giselle is in marketing and events planning. "She's got resources, she knows people, I know people—we got our people together, " says Choki, describing her relationship with Giselle as stemming from mutual chemistry, each bringing their own resources to the relationship to give birth to Urban Voices.

Choki hopes that her cooperative spirit with Giselle will extend to people coming together at future Urban Voices forums. As much as she hopes the events are about entertainment, she also hopes they allow a joining of like-minded individuals in the same place with freedom to positively exchange ideas. She calls this "networking made easier."

"We are one, and this is not meant to be said as a slogan or banner, for one to exploit one another, we are powerful as one diverse, one nation, one continent, one people, one, one, one AFRICA! But the battle has only begun," raps Burni.

It takes a lot of guts to get up in front of the masses and express yourself, says Choki, who adds that Urban Voices is not an officially registered company. In the future Choki and Giselle say they hope to create a membership, a following, and develop a permanent forum where young people can exercise their democratic right to freedom of expression.

Choki says she thinks the popularity of spoken-word and poetry performance has increased in the last few years. Though she says this particular event is not breaking even, it did attract fifty-three people, plus others dining in the Ikhaya African Restaurant—a promising start.

"It's social consciousness on some level. I might be walking out of a club at 3 a.m., and this person is still begging. And how much money have I been pissing? The reality is: rich is rich, and poor poorer. Every day people get wet because they need to eat," she says, as if practicing for her own debut.

# APPENDICES

# SIMMONS COLLEGE

Simmons College is a nationally distinguished, small university in the heart of Boston, Massachusetts, with a 2006/2007 enrollment of 5,000. Founded in 1899, Simmons was the first four-year college in the United States to provide both liberal arts and career preparation for women. Today, it has undergraduate programs for women and graduate programs for women and men, including the world's only graduate business program designed specifically for women; co-ed graduate schools of library and information science, health studies, and social work; and co-ed graduate programs in education, communications management and liberal arts.

## ACADEMICS

The undergraduate College of Arts and Sciences, from which the participants in the South Africa project are drawn, has close to 2,000 students, more than a fifth of whom are self-identified members of ethnic minorities. The school is best known for its distinctive emphasis on preprofessional education that prepares students for the working world. It combines a traditional liberal arts education with courses tailored to the students' future vocations. Students are also required to take interdisciplinary courses in the areas of writing, art, literature, language, history, scientific inquiry, quantitative reasoning and ethics, among others.

Simmons offers degrees in a wide range of disciplines, with more than forty majors and programs. Among the most popular are psychology, communications, political science/international relations, nursing, management, biology/pre-med and English. Interdisciplinary majors include Africana and women's studies. Distinguished faculty include noted researchers, authors, and experts who are passionately dedicated to teaching. While the curriculum is challenging, small classes and a collaborative environment facilitate student success.

Students expand classroom work and prepare for the world after college through independent study, usually an internship. The requirement—a hallmark of a Simmons education—challenges them to approach a problem, project or workplace experience as independent researchers and applied learners. This gives them a rigorous intellectual experience that enables them to attain both depth and practice in their chosen disciplines, to sustain a longer-term project of their own initiative, and to connect their academic work with future employment or graduate study.

Students acquire a global outlook by studying languages, cultures, and foreign policies and by taking advantage of foreign study opportunities, including intensive "short courses," such as the one to South Africa, and half- or full-year programs. Simmons is a member of the Colleges of the Fenway consortium, which also includes Wentworth Institute of Technology, Wheelock College, Emmanuel College, Massachusetts College of Pharmacy and Health Sciences, and the Massachusetts College of Art. The New England Philharmonic is the College's orchestra-in-residence.

## CAMPUS LIFE

Boston, the largest and oldest of the New England region's many cities, is rich in history, tradition and cultural diversity. It attracts more than 250,000 undergraduate and graduate students from around the world every year, making it the nation's largest "college town." As an urban institution deeply involved in and committed to the city, Simmons places many students in field-based work at neighborhood institutions as part of their regular courses of study. Fully thirty percent participate in off-campus service learning.

Simmons is located between Boston's lively Fenway district and the Longwood Medical Area, a world-renowned hub for research and health care. Eighty-eight percent of students live on campus in nine residence halls. They take advantage of a vibrant urban community of colleges, research centers, museums, sports stadiums, restaurants, shops, and performance venues in a neighborhood that is the soul of the city.

College women compete in eight NCAA Division III varsity intercollegiate sports: basketball, crew, field hockey, soccer, swimming, diving, tennis, and volleyball. Simmons also belongs to the Great Northeast Athletic Conference (GNAC) and the Eastern Collegiate Athletic Conference (ECAC) and is affiliated with the Massachusetts Association of Intercollegiate Athletics for Women (MAIAW).

A wide variety of academic and other campus organizations involve students of all types. Academic clubs appeal to students interested in communications, psychology, biology/pre-med, math/computer science, and other fields. Other organizations include language and culture, performing arts, student government, honor societies, publications, entertainment, international and multicultural student associations, religious groups, and community service opportunities.

## S.A. TRIP ACADEMIC SPONSORS

The fifteen-person student group that produced the articles for this book did so for an advanced feature-writing course in the Department of Communications. The Departments of Political Science/International Relations and Women's Studies also accredited the course toward their majors.

## DEPARTMENT OF COMMUNICATIONS

The mission of the Department of Communications is to provide an intellectually broadening path of study of the media, and preparation for the communications profession. Faculty are committed to standards of excellence and to the creation of a climate where students strive to make a difference in the community. The program emphasizes the development of critical thinking and problem-solving, superior writing capabilities, a contemporary visual intelligence, effective oral communication, and technical competence in the digital age.

Students actively engage with the challenge of communication for the screen, the page, and the World Wide Web while gaining an understanding of the impact of the media on society and the individual, and the influence of media convergence on the practice of communications. These objectives are accomplished by a supportive environment of collaboration, creativity, and active engagement with experiential learning led by a faculty of professionals and scholars.

The communications major provides a foundation in the study of written, visual, and electronic media. Areas of specialization allow students to take developmental coursework in one area within the field. This program culminates in advanced coursework and capstone experiences like internships, independent study, and Studio 5—the department's student-run, professional communications workplace that designed and laid out this book.

The major prepares students for employment in a great variety of positions dealing with communications-related problems and opportunities that face contemporary businesses and organizations. Typical career paths include publishing, print and broadcast journalism, public relations, advertising, video, graphic, Web, and multimedia design and production.

## DEPARTMENT OF POLITICAL SCIENCE/INTERNATIONAL RELATIONS

Part of a liberal arts education is exposure to a plurality of perspectives and values, and an encouragement of civil and rational discourse amidst fundamental disagreement. The Department of Political Science and International Relations offers two majors designed toward these ends.

The political science curriculum includes a senior integrative seminar where students reflect on how the major subfields and ideological approaches of the discipline relate to a common topic. The capstone integrative seminar for international relations majors, taught by a distinguished practitioner in international affairs who holds the "Warburg Chair in International Relations," encourages students to combine conceptual and content-based knowledge with policy applications. This major encourages responsible world citizenship that recognizes both the historically and politically contingent nature of geographic and political divisions, and the perennial dilemmas of theorizing beyond borders.

Both majors gain real-life experience through internships in legislative and governmental offices, domestic and international NGOs, and the international sectors of various corporations and financial institutions. In 2004, for example, twelve students studied the American presidential selection process throughout the spring term (via on-line assignments and discussions) and then spent an intense two weeks at the Democratic National Convention in Boston in hands-on activities and internships.

The department also administers the new Barbara Lee Fellows Program, which attracts strong students from several majors who compete for fellowships leading to mentoring relationships with area legislators, and it supports study and interning abroad, with faculty members taking students on foreign study experiences to Egypt, Thailand, China, and Japan, and working to foster links across the College like those that paired communications and political science and international relations students in the South Africa project.

## DEPARTMENT OF WOMEN'S STUDIES

The Department of Women's Studies helps students develop theoretical, empirical, and methodological perspectives for studying the history, status and experiences of women. By considering women and gender in diverse national and international contexts, students study the multiple and contested meanings and roles of gender to develop an understanding of how gender is related to other social categories such as race, class, age, sexuality, religion, and nationality.

Women's studies students frequently combine a major or minor in women's studies with a second major, such as communications, sociology, philosophy, psychology, or political science, which prepares them for a wide range of careers. Courses, whether taken as part of a major, or to enrich another discipline, invite students to understand past and present experiences in order to prepare for challenges and opportunities in their future personal, work, and social lives.

The department also administers a social justice minor, developed with Africana Studies and Sociology, for students with a particular interest in activism. As with internships or independent learning in women's studies, students gain experience in real-life situations in community-based organizations that focus on issues of social justice. Two women's studies majors were part of the South Africa project.

# THE ITINERARY:
# MAY 16 – JUNE 6

## ■ JOHANNESBURG

**MONDAY, MAY 16**

Arrival in South Africa.

Informal meeting/dinner at the Rosebank Hotel with students from the University of Witwatersrand (Wits).

**TUESDAY, MAY 17**

Morning tour of Soweto township with visits to the flea market and the Nelson Mandela Museum; lunch at Wandi's eatery at Dube Village; a visit to the Hector Petierson Museum and a school for the disabled; and a resident-led walk-through of cramped two- and three-room homes.

Late afternoon seminar at Wits with journalism department chair and former *Weekly Mail* editor Anton Harber.

**WEDNESDAY, MAY 18**

Morning excursion to Ormonde for a half-day visit to the Apartheid Museum.

Afternoon seminar at COSATU on the role of trade unions in the freedom struggle and women in the unions led by National Gender Coordinator Mummy Jafta and Education Department head Pongani Masuku.

Evening roundtable on "Black Empowerment and African Women in Business" led by former Women's National Coalition chair Thandi Marah with panelists Nhlanna Mioli-Mncuba, Nothemba Mlonzi and Mpumi Majavu.

**THURSDAY, MAY 19**

Morning seminar on "Gender in the New South Africa" at the Wiser Institute at Wits with panelists Detlev Krige, Grace Khunou and Kgamadi Kometski.

Afternoon visit to the Limpho Hani Child Care Centre for AIDS orphans in Doornkop, Soweto, arranged by Wits professor Sheila Meintjes and guided by crèche volunteer Gill Goodall and crèche director Nthabiseng Hlongwane.

Late afternoon lecture/slide show by Professor Connell at the Wiser Institute on "Redeeming the Failed Promise of Democracy in Eritrea."

Evening roundtable on "Women in the Media" organized by US embassy public affairs staff with panelists Karema Brown, Mpho Moagi, and Cornia Pretorius.

FRIDAY, MAY 20

A guided morning tour of Constitution Hill and the Constitutional Court set up by Wits professor Barbara Buntman.

An afternoon tour of the Museum Africa in the Newtown Cultural Precinct.

Dinner at Gramadoelas with traditional Afrikaner dishes.

Evening at the Market Theatre to see Julian Seleke-Mokoto's "Shattered Dreams."

SATURDAY, MAY 21

Visit to the Funda Community College in Soweto with Wits fine arts professor David Andrews. Presenters included director Charles Nkosi and artists Nelsie Ndimande, Ntombifuthi Sangweni, Thuli Bhengu, Lorraine Ndlovu and Pauline Mazibuko.

Evening *brai* (South African barbeque) with Wits students and friends.

SUNDAY, MAY 22

Visit to rooftop market at Rosebank.

MONDAY, MAY 23

Departure on overnight Shosholoza Meyl train for Cape Town.

# ■ CAPE TOWN

**TUESDAY, MAY 24**

Arrival in mid-afternoon; tour of the Victoria and Albert Waterfront.

**WEDNESDAY, MAY 25**

A guided city tour of Cape Town including a visit to the old Slave Lodge, the Company Gardens, the Iziko Museum (formerly the South Africa Museum), the Castle of Good Hope and Table Mountain via cable car.

Afternoon group reflection at the Breakwater Lodge.

**THURSDAY, MAY 26**

Morning Parliament briefing hosted by ANC MP Jeremy Cronin, featuring ANC women MPs Connie September and Ncumisa Kondlo.

Late morning embassy briefing at the U.S. Consulate.

Noon jazz concert at the University of Cape Town College of Music, followed by an informal afternoon session with women musician.

Evening program at Iziko with lecture and slides on Eritrea by Prof. Connell.

**FRIDAY, MAY 27**

A full-day township tour including a walk through the Malay community at Bo-Kaap led by Tana Baru Tours director and former underground ANC activist Shereen Habib; a visit to the District 6 Museum; and meetings with leaders of the South African Homeless Peoples Federation who led a walk-through of women-constructed houses in the Victoria Mahlenge township.

**SATURDAY, MAY 28**

Africa Day Festival in the City Garden.

**SUNDAY, MAY 29**

Free day.

MONDAY, MAY 30

A full-day excursion to the Cape of Good Hope, including Cape of Good Hope Nature Reserve and the Cape penguin colony at Boulders Beach.

TUESDAY, MAY 31

Morning orientation on HIV/AIDS in South Africa by Treatment Action Campaign provincial coordinator Thembeka Majali at her Salt River office, followed by a visit to the JL Zwane Centre and a workshop with TAC community activists.

Afternoon visit to TAC offices in Khayelitsha township with discussion among TAC organizers and leaders of Positive Men United and Positive Women United.

WEDNESDAY, JUNE 1

A half-day excursion to Robben Island, where Nelson Mandela and other anti-apartheid activists spent more than a quarter of a century in prison.

Afternoon writing workshop at the Breakwater Lodge.

Evening excursion to see Mike van Graan's "Green Man Flashing" at UCT's Baxter Theatre.

THURSDAY, JUNE 2

Tour of the Saartjie Baartman Centre for Women and Children led by director Ilse Ahrends and a briefing on community groups housed there (Muslim AIDS Project, Rape Crisis, Trauma Centre, Saartjie Baartman Shelter, Western Cape Network on Violence Against Women).

FRIDAY, JUNE 3

Independent research and small-group interviews, including Talia Sanhewe, assistant producer of SABC's "Otherwise—the women's perspective on SAfm."

SATURDAY, JUNE 4

Independent research and small-group interviews.

## SUNDAY, JUNE 5

Departure for Boston.

# CONTACTS IN SOUTH AFRICA

## ■ JOHANNESBURG

### JOURNALISM DEPARTMENT SEMINAR
University of the Witwatersrand (Wits)
Private Bag 3
Wits 2050, S.A.
http://www.wits.ac.za

Anton Harber, Dept. Chair —anton@harber.co.za

### CONGRESS OF SOUTH AFRICAN TRADE UNIONS (COSATU)
COSATU House
1 Leyds Street
Braamfontein 2000, S.A.
http://www.cosatu.org.za/

Mummy Jafta, Gender Coordinator
Pongani Masuku, Education Dept. Director

### "WOMEN IN BUSINESS" SEMINAR
Thandi Marah—Thandi.marah@eskom.co.za
Nhlannla Mjoli-Mncube—nhlannlam@wol.co.za
Nothemba Mlonzi—mlonzi@mweb.co.za
Mpumi Majavu—majavu@tiscali.co.za

### "GENDER IN SOUTH AFRICA" SEMINAR
Wiser Institute
University of the Witwatersrand
Private Bag 3
Wits 2050, S.A.
http://wiserweb.wits.ac.za

Deborah Posel, Director—poseld@wiser.wits.ac.za
Detlev Krige—kriged@wiser.wits.ac.za
Grace Khunou—khunoug@wiser.wits.ac.za
Kgamadi Kometsi—kometsik@wiser.wits.ac.za

## LIMPHO HANI CHILD CARE CENTRE
## DOORNKOP, SOWETO
c/o Dr. Sheila Meintjes
Dept of Political Studies
University of the Witwatersrand
Private Bag 3
Wits 2050, S.A.

Nthabiseng Hlongwane, Founder/director
Sheila Meintjes, Wits advisor—meintjess@social.wits.ac.za

## "WOMEN IN MEDIA" SEMINAR
Karema Brown—brownk@bdfm.co.za
Mpho Moagi—moagicm@sabc.co.za
Cornia Pretorius—cpretori@beeld.com

## FUNDA COMMUNITY COLLEGE
P.O. Box 2056
Southdale 2135, S.A.

Charles Nkosi, Founder/director
David Andrews, Wits advisor—andrewd@artworks.wits.ac.za
Nelsie Ndimande, Artist
Ntombifuthi Sangweni, Artist
Thuli Bhengu, Artist
Lorraine Ndlovu, Artist
Pauline Mazibuko, Artist

# ■ CAPE TOWN
## JEDEK TRAVEL
4 Struben Road
Claremont 7700, S.A.
http://www.jedek.com

Thana Nel, Director—thana@jedek.com

## MEMBERS OF PARLIAMENT

National Assembly
Parliament Road
Cape Town 8000, S.A.
Jeremy Cronin—jcronin@anc.org.za
Connie September—carolseptember@worldonline.co.za
Ncumisa Kondlo

## U.S. CONSULATE—CAPE TOWN

P.O. Box 6773
Roggebaai 8012, S.A.

Contact—consularcapetown@state.gov

## COLLEGE OF MUSIC
## UNIVERSITY OF CAPE TOWN (UCT)

Private Bag
Rondebosch 7701, S.A.
http://www.uct.ac.za

Paul Sedres, Music Lab—Sedresp@PROTEM.uct.ac.za

## IZIKO (FORMERLY SOUTH AFRICA MUSEUM)

25 Queen Victoria Street
Cape Town 8000, S.A.
http://www.museums.org.za/sam

Vivienne Carelse, Director—vcarelse@iziko.org.za

## TANA BARU TOURS (BO KAAP)

3 Morris Street
Schotschekloof
Cape Town 8001, S.A.
http://www.tanabarutours.co.za/

Shereen Habib, Director—tanabarutours@webmail.co.za

## S.A. HOMELESS PEOPLE'S FEDERATION

Cape Town, S.A.
http://www.dialogue.org.za/
Rose Maso, Victoria Mahlenge township

## TAC NATIONAL OFFICE
34 Main Road
Muizenberg 7945, S.A.
http://www.tac.org.za/

Rukia Cornelius, contact—info@tac.org.za
Sipho Mthathi, contact

## TAC PROVINCIAL OFFICE
Community House
41 Salt River Road
Salt River 7925
Cape Town, S.A.

Thembeka Majali—thembeka@tac.org.za

## TAC KHAYELITSHA
A760 A, Site C
Khayelitsha 7789
Cape Town, S.A.

Mandla Majola, contact
Isaac Magwala (Positive Men United)
Noncedo Bulana (Positive Women United)

## SAARTJIE BAARTMAN CENTRE FOR WOMEN & CHILDREN
PO Box 38401
Gatesville 7764, S.A.
saartjiebaartman@womenscentre.co.za

Ilse Ahrends, Director—ilse@womenscentre.co.za

Also:
Muslim AIDS Project
Shahieda Allie, Director—mapwcape@mweb.co.za

Rape Crisis
Chantel Cooper, Director—chantel@rapecrisis.org.za

Trauma Centre
Haseena Parker, Counselor—haseena@trauma.org.za

Saartjie Baartman Shelter
Rosemarie Cox, Manager—rose@womenscentre.co.za

Western Cape Network on Violence Against Women
Cheryl Ayogu, Director—Cheryl@womenscentre.co.za

## OTHERWISE - THE WOMAN'S PERSPECTIVE ON SAFM

Broadcast 7.30-8pm Monday to Friday
Sea Point, Cape Town, S.A.
http://www.safm.co.za
otherwise@safm.co.za

Talia Sanhewe, assistant producer—sanhewest@sabc.co.za

# NOTES ON THE CONTRIBUTORS

**Dan Connell**, the author of six books and the founder and former director of the Boston-based aid agency Grassroots International, teaches journalism and African politics at Simmons College. His reports and commentary have been carried by the BBC, Voice of America, AP, Reuters, *The Boston Globe*, *The Miami Herald*, *The Washington Post*, *The Guardian*, *Le Monde*, *Foreign Affairs*, *The Nation*, and other print and broadcast media, and he has consulted for numerous aid agencies and human rights organizations.

— —

**Alexandria Carithers**, a senior from Boston, Mass., is majoring in biology and minoring in chemistry in a pre-med program. She sits on the executive board of the Black Student Organization and is a peer educator with Sex at Simmons. She is also interning at Brigham and Women's hospital in the teratology department and she aspires to a career in obstetrics and gynecology.

> *"I was floored at how similar the socioeconomic problems in South Africa are to those in the U.S. for people of African descent."* — Alexandria Carithers

**Amanda Cary**, a senior from Simsbury, Conn., designed her own major in International Health, focusing on health issues in the developing world. After graduation she plans to join the Peace Corps for two years and then to pursue graduate studies in the field of international health.

**Jennifer Daniels**, a senior from Birnanwood, Wisc.., is an International Relations major who spent a semester abroad in Amman, Jordan.

> *"Prejudices based on race, class and gender exist in both our nations. South Africans are just more willing to admit it."* — Justine DeLuca

**Justine Deluca**, a senior from Pittsfield, Mass., is an International Relations major with a focus in conflict resolution and diplomacy. She is the president and volunteer coordinator for Simmons Community Outreach, a volunteer for Habitat for Humanity, a Student Advisor on Multiculturalism, and the coordinator of the Simmons chapter of Students Taking Action Now: Darfur and the College's observance of World AIDS Day.

**Christine Franey**, a senior from Burlington, Mass., is a member of the Honors Program double-majoring in Chemistry and Mathematics. A participant in the National Science Foundation's 2004 "Women in Material Science" program, she has spent summers in NSF-sponsored seminars and research programs at the Universities of Connecticut and Wisconsin. She is a campus tutor at Simmons and plans to pursue a career in public health.

> *"The experience was unforgettable and cemented my desire to attend graduate school in public health."*
> – Christine Franey

**Renee Frojo**, a sophomore from Auburn, Alabama, is a Communications major, with a concentration in writing, and an International Relations minor. She is a member of the Student Government Association and a columnist for the weekly campus newspaper *The Simmons Voice*. She spends summers teaching international relations at the National Student Leadership Conference in Washington, D.C., and she has spent a semester abroad in Rome, Italy.

**Evan S. Kuhlman**, a senior from Cincinnati, Ohio, is double-majoring in Women's Studies and Communications with a dual concentration in public relations and writing. She has served as the features and layout editor and editor-in-chief of the weekly campus newspaper *The Simmons Voice* and the semi-annual literary magazine *Sidelines*. She also directs the campus Women's Center and is a member of Student Government Association, Communications Liaison and Public Relations Student Society of America.

**Kate Lolley**, a 2005 Simmons graduate from Vineyard Haven, Mass., majored in Biology in the pre-med program and took a Society and Health minor. She now works at Brigham and Women's Hospital, Boston.

> *"The spirit of the South African people through so many struggles is an inspiration to the rest of the world."* – Kathryn McCarthy

**Kathryn McCarthy**, a junior from North Reading, Mass., is majoring in Nursing and minoring in Biology. She is a member of Simmons Community Outreach and the Nursing Liaison. One of her South Africa articles appeared in *The North Reading Transcript*, for which she reported while in high school.

**Gina Patterson**, a senior from West Bridgewater, Mass., is double-majoring in Biopsychology and Women's Studies. She is the president of the Black Students Organization and has served as a member of the Student Government Association executive board, a Firstyear Facilitator, and the chair of Student Advisors for Multiculturalism. She has participated in numerous panels on diversity and is a volunteer for the Dudley Street Neighborhood Initiative.

> *"Women in South Africa are courageous, strong and fearless—a definite 'rock' in their society."* – Gina Patterson

**Erin Rook**, a senior from McMinnville, Oregon, is majoring in Communications, with a concentration in writing. She has served as the opinion and arts and entertainment editor and editor-in-chief of the weekly campus newspaper *The Simmons Voice* and is president of the Communications Liaison. She spent a year in South Africa before attending Simmons College where she was a group facilitator for the South African Youth Enrichment Programme.

**Fay Stambuk**, a junior from Germany/Croatia, is double-majoring in International Relations and Management, with a minor in Economics. Her IR concentration focuses on development studies, particularly in Africa. She is the president of the International Multicultural Student Association, a member of the Student Advisors on Multiculturalism, and a senator for the Economics Liaison. Her extracurricular activities reflect her interest in promoting internationalism and diversity.

**Lyly Tran**, a senior from South Kingston, R.I., is a member of the Honors Program majoring in Biochemistry and International Relations with a concentration in development. She is also the president of the Asian Students Association and an intern at the Harvard Institutes of Medicine. She aspires to work as a physician in developing countries, particularly Vietnam and South Africa, both of which she has visited.

> *"Studying abroad opened my eyes to a world larger than I ever imagined. The experience was life-changing."* – Darline Tunis

**Darline Tunis**, a junior from Randolph, Mass., is a member of the Honors Program majoring in Economics and minoring in English. She sits on the executive boards of the Student Government Association and the Black Student Organization and is a Resident Adviser. She is also the multicultural intern in the Office of Undergraduate Admissions.

**Lindsey Varney,** is a 2005 Simmons graduate from West Chester, Penn., with a degree in Marketing and Economics. Courses such as Management in the Diverse Workforce and Writing Across the Media peaked her interest as a student. She also volunteered at the annual Simmons School of Management Women's Leadership Conferences. She is currently in New York City pursuing a career in advertising.

> *"Meeting ordinary people who had such an impact on their society made me feel really proud and motivated me to learn more about South Africa."*– Lindsey Varney